The Sassy Way to

SOCIAL

MEDIA

Marketing

~~~~~

when you have NO CLUE...

by Gundi Gabrielle

First Edition Paperback: March 2017

ISBN-13: 978-1544628776
ISBN-10: 1544628773

The Cataloging-In-Publication Data is on file with the Library of Congress.

*This is a **SassyZenGirl** Guide*

FREE Bonus

Hi there!

Great to meet you! - I am excited to help you grow your following on Social Media.

As a *thank you* for purchasing my book, I prepared a FREE report that's exclusive to you, my readers.

WORDS THAT SELL

The Psychology behind the 10 most Influential Words in the English Language and how you can use them to Grow Your Following and turn Readers into Buyers

Just go to:

SassyZenGirl.com/Social-Media-Report

Enjoy!

Gundi Gabrielle

PS: you will also receive a free subscription to my lifestyle blog SassyZenGirl and if that's not for you, no worries, you can unsubscribe immediately after you receive your free report. Just click the "unsubscribe" link at the bottom of the welcome email.

TABLE OF CONTENTS

Chapter 1 - First things First....

Welcome - and great to see you!

I'm excited to share some awesome features and marketing strategies to help you grow your following on the 5 major social networks - Youtube, Facebook, Twitter, Instagram and Pinterest.

We will start with the two visual networks: Instagram and Pinterest, followed by the evergreens Facebook and Twitter, before closing with a massive chapter on Youtube.

Ready to begin?

Then here we go!

Staggering Numbers

In case you weren't aware….;-) - the number of people using social media on a daily basis is staggering!

Just look at the the number of monthly visitors for each platform as of January 2017:

Facebook - 1, 860,000,000
Youtube - 1,000,000,000
Instagram - 600,000,000
Twitter - 313,000,000
Pinterest - 150,000,000

Also notable: the trend towards video has greatly expanded with *live video* on Facebook, Twitter and Instagram and is expected to explode even more in 2017.

In fact, Alexa ranking of most popular websites lists Youtube *before* Facebook at #2, right after Google!

Social Media Strategies

In this introductory chapter, we will cover the overall marketing strategies that apply to all social media, including ways to monetize your profiles and tools that are helpful to all.

I will be sharing a lot of resources and occasionally link out to relevant Youtube videos for visual context. For this reason, I created a resource page with direct links, so you don't have to type them all in.

Just enter this url on your computer or iPad and keep it open while reading this book.

SassyZenGirl.com/Social-Media-Resources

How to use this Book

The topic of this book is marketing. As such, we will not go over the technical aspects of setting up your profiles or how to use each platform, except for specific features.

There are plenty of Youtube tutorials that will quickly take you through the basics and answer any question you might have.

Each chapter will start with a brief overview of what makes each platform unique as well as current and upcoming trends.

This is followed by the marketing aspects of:

- *Your Profile*
- *Your Posts/videos*
- *Multiple strategies to grow your Following*
- *Monetization*

At the end of each chapter you will find a list of:

- *Tools & Additional Training*

to help you grow further and a suggested

- *Daily Routine*

to help you get organized in the beginning.

Upcoming Trends

Social Media are an ever changing world of buzz and intrigue. This also affects your marketing. What may have worked 2 years ago, may no longer be valid, and it's important to stay up to date with trends and changes for each platform.

I recommend reading the following 2 articles by two of the top sources for anything related to Social Media marketing, featuring their predictions for 2017 (see Resources page):

Social Media Examiner
Buffer

Now, lets begin…..

Strategies for Success

In this section, we will cover general marketing concepts and strategies that are relevant to all social media platforms.

While you are probably eager to get to the network chapters and start posting like a champ....;-) - please don't overlook this part.

It may not be as glamorous as becoming a social media rockstar, but these are the foundations that can make it happen for you.

Ignore them and chances are you will get lost in the million of other similar pages that try to do the exact same thing you do.

Chapter is about the foundation, the "bread and butter strategies both for your business and social media presence.

Get that set up properly from the start and you will have a much better chance at succeeding.

Those are the strategies that the top influencers on each platform have used to build their following and you can do the same.

...are you ready?

Build a Brand, not a Profile

This is the most important one!

Skip this part and you might as well not start at all.

Before you do anything else, you need to become crystal clear on the following 3 points:

1) Your VISION
What are you hoping to achieve with your business or blog? What are your goals? WHY are you running this business or service? (and just "making money" isn't enough...;-)

What is driving you emotionally? Inspires you?

That's what will get you through the frustrating times that everyone experiences once in a while.

WHY do you do what you do?

The more clearly you can answer those questions, the clearer your vision for your business - and your social media strategy - will become.

2) Your "Unique VALUE Proposition"
Ok….that's a bit of a tongue breaker….;-) - but a classic marketing term that's incredibly important…

Basically, it means - how do you/your brand add value to people's lives?

WHY would they follow you?

What do you offer that others don't? What is your specific angle? Your niche or sub niche?

What problem, pain, frustration or need do you solve for your audience?

And *how* do you solve it?

In short, you need to answer the #1 question on every potential client's mind:

What's in it for me?

3) Your Target AUDIENCE
Define exactly who your target audience is.

Male/female, age range, profession, marital status, location, interests, goals, dreams, problems/ challenges...

What drives them and what do they need?

What are their problems, worries or frustrations that you can help alleviate?
Or maybe you bring joy, entertainment - or inspiration?

Where do they hang out (online)?
How do you find them/connect with them?

It's helpful to actually write down a profile of one prototype in your audience. A little fictional bio of someone who embodies all those traits.

THAT will be the "person" you will tailor your content and marketing to.

Speak to that person directly, specifically, and it will greatly transform everything you do from here on out.

Your Elevator Pitch....

Take some time to become really clear on the above 3 points and try to define your brand in 1 concise sentence:

What is your Brand?
What problems does it solve for your audience? and Who it is for?

-> your elevator pitch.

You only have to do this once and can then apply it whatever platforms you choose.

Take some time with this step. It's actually really fu and your future marketing will be so much mo targeted and on point.

It doesn't have to perfect. It will probably still evolve over time - it certainly did for me with the

SassyZenGirl brand - but starting the process now as best you can will give you the most important ingredient for success:

FOCUS!

Putting it all together....

Once you have clearly defined your brand, the next fun step - and it *can* be really fun and exciting! - is developing your social media *strategy*.

This is where this book can help you - first, by introducing the different platforms and showing their features and possibilities.

Everyone is familiar with Facebook, but few people know Pinterest or even Instagram, which is why I put them first.

They are both amazingly powerful marketing machines and much easier for growing a following than say Facebook (due to Facebook's restrictive algorithm).

If you are artistic, spiritual or love beautiful things and pictures, you will LOVE - and thrive - on these platforms, so I invite you to at least have a look before jumping right into Facebook and Twitter.

Facebook is of course, the main staple and everyone should have a Facebook business page, but don't limit yourself just because it's more familiar.

Using Pinterest and Instagram is easy and after a short learning curve you can really have fun there and see your following grow quickly.

Youtube features a *massive* chapter which is why I put it last.

The very nature of a video platform requires more steps - but also many more possibilities for generating an income!

Youtube is amazing in that regard and it ain' just comin' from ads as you might thinl ..

If tech stuff scares you, don't let it to you!

Find a tech savvy high school kid th t wants to make a few extra bucks and have him take care of the filming and editing while you focus on creating great content.

Or you partner with someone of similar interest and grow your channel - and online presence - together.

Youtube is awesome! - and a totally new way of connecting with your audience.

You don't even have to be on camera. You can do how-to or product videos (for affiliate marketing) and record your screen (very easy!).

I invite you to at least *consider* Youtube as a platform and not be too concerned about technical hurdles.

It is the absolute powerhouse of Internet marketing!

Sooo……..

Once you have a clear vision for your brand, you can then decide which platforms you want to add to your social media portfolio - and in what capacity.

They shouldn't all cover the same as many of your fans will eventually follow you on all or at least several.

Plus, each platform is good for specific things, so finding a strategy that complements them all is what you are looking for.

Start with one

Social Media marketing is very involved and requires regular posting of high quality content.

This can be exhausting at times unless you get a good routine going and employ management tools for scheduling etc.

It's best to start with only one or two platforms and spend all your efforts on growing a following there. Once that's "flying" and you have found your groove, you add the next.

It's much better to be VERY successful on one platform than getting burnt out while trying them all.

Now lets go over 1) important marketing strategies and habits that apply to all social media platforms, before we finally explore each individually - bear with me...;-)

#1 - A Cohesive Strategy

Your marketing efforts will be much more effective if you cross promote and connect your platforms as well as your website.

Interlink your profiles, e.g. have a direct link to all your other social networks on each profile (wherever possible).

Frequently share from one platform to another and invite people to join you.

Place social media widgets on your website, e.g. "Follow"/"Subscribe" buttons and - where possible - profile widgets that show your recent posts.

#2 - Consistency & Quality

Growing a social media following only works if you consistently provide high quality content. Facebook and Pinterest already rank by quality and not chronology, and no one will allow you into their timeline for long unless you have something valuable to add.

Common sense, right?

Quality also means researching what your followers actually *want* to see and are interested in, not what you *think* they want to see.

Following the top performers and hot trends in your field will give you a first good sense.

Platforms like **BuzzSumo** and **Feedly** are further great resources.

And, of course, you should *ask* your audience from time to time them or take a poll. You might be surprised at the answers….

As for consistency - from observing the top influencers on each platform, it's obvious they all post a LOT.

And day after day.

So how to not get overwhelmed…
The more you post, the more chances of people finding your content - that's simple mathematics.

It can feel overwhelming in the beginning and that's why starting with just one or two platforms is better than getting burned out by five.

Fortunately, there are scheduling and management tools like **SocialSprout** and **PostPlanner** that can greatly streamline the process and save you time.

Also, bulk producing 10-20 pieces of content and then uploading them into the above scheduling platforms will save you time and keep you organized.

You can spend 1 day researching content, another day creating the posts and then an hour or so setting up scheduling - all for the next week, or even month.

It will take a little time to get your groove, but once you do, it will be quite easy to do this on the side without overwhelming everything else in your life.

#3 - Engage

Social Media are just that - social!

It's about communicating, sharing, networking - not a one way street of just posting.

You always want to engage with others - and your followers in particular.

Ask questions, their opinions etc. (more on that under #4 "Call to Action")

Also, try to respond to comments, messages, retweets etc. in a timely manner.

You also need to actively follow others in your niche and comment, share, like *their* content. NOT for self promotion (e.g. asking people to check out your page with a link - BIG no-no, that can easily get you banned!), but with genuine interest, actually reading what they share and giving intelligent feedback.

This is about networking and getting on people's radar. If you do this consistently, people will want to check out your profile without a spammy sales pitch from you.

Give first! - Give a lot of value and help, as much as you can, and people will start noticing you and check out your stuff.

And…..if you have great content to offer, they will certainly stick around.

The same goes for influencers with large followings. Their endorsement can bring a huge sudden growth to your entire brand, but you have to earn it.

Do the above and don't expect any reaction at first. Over time though, they will notice you if you gradually build that relationship.

#4 - Include a Call to Action

In that same line, wherever possible, end your posts with a "Call-to-Action" (CTA). This can be a request to answer a question or share an opinion in the comments, tag someone, share, like - and occasionally click on a link.

Try to engage your audience with every post.

It will make a huge difference in your engagement ratio and make it fun to follow you.

You also show that you care and don't just put out information. Start the conversation, that's what social media is all about: communicating, sharing, participating - not lecturing.

The more you do, the faster you can grow.

#5 - A compelling Profile

This is a big one and you need to start there. Your profile is often the first thing visitors see and check out before deciding to follow you.

It defines your brand and is your first introduction to someone who has never heard of you.

Always put good care into crafting a great one.

#6 - Contests & Giveaways

Contests and giveaways are a fun way to create on buzz and get people interested in your brand.

Entry requirements can include a follow, a share, a shoutout, leaving a review, signing up to your list, or any other combination.

If the prize is good, people will want to participate and also actively share your invitation - > additional exposure to people who otherwise might have never seen you.

Wishpond is a great contest management tool that makes the process easy.

#7 - Guest Posting

A powerful and quick way to attract interest in your business and social media platforms!

That's when you get invited to write an article for a big blog with a large and active following. The exposure from such posts can be enormous and you can mention your social media profiles in the short author bio at the end.

Even long after publishing, people can still find your articles for months and years to come through Google searches. Every guest post can generate a continuous stream of new followers to all your platforms and your website.

Landing great guest posts is difficult in the beginning, but not impossible and really a short cut to growing your following quickly.

You need to know:

- how to write: there is a particular style to good blogging and great headlines
- what topics to pick - and most of all -
- how to pitch your articles to big blogs

There is a fantastic online course by Jon Morrow, one of the most successful bloggers in the world who as a freelancer was paid up to $7,000 per article and now runs his own 7-figure blog.

The course teaches you all the above in just a few short weeks and comes with a rolodex ("Black Book") of editor emails to more than 100 top level blogs, incl. The Huffington Post, Forbes, and Fast Company.

This link will give you access at a 35% Discount. You can also find it in the Resources section:

SassyZenGirl.com/Guest-Blogging

#8 - Kindle Publishing

Just as powerful as guest posting - if not more so!

Being a "Published Author" - or even a "Bestselling Author" - comes with great prestige.

You are instantly perceived as an authority in your field.

More importantly, you are tapping into the marketing power of the biggest online store in the world - Amazon!

And….it is one of the easiest and fastest ways to grow a following - both for your blog/business and your social media.

You get new followers on auto-pilot - and you even get paid for it!

Book #5 in this series will cover the ins and outs of Kindle Publishing and how to publish your first bestseller in 30 days…..

#9 - Watch your Analytics

Keep an eye on your analytics. Each social media platform offers an analytics page with:

- data on your audience demographics
- which posts got the most engagement and
- how well your page is growing.

These will be invaluable insights and help you fine tune your campaigns. Check your analytics regularly and adjust where needed.

#10 - Build your Mailing List

Email marketing far outranks any other type of marketing, even Facebook or Google Ads.

More importantly, you own and control that list. No one can take it from you - unlike social platforms who could always ban you or change their rules.

You can use your social networks to build that list by occasionally linking out to a "landing page".

What's a landing page?

It's a sub page on your website dedicated solely to the purpose of collecting someone's email.

No distractions, no menu or side bar, just an offer - usually a free report, eBook or discount - that visitors can access by giving you their email address.

You've seen them many times and if the offer was appealing and something you really wanted, you probably signed up.

If you want to see what a landing page looks like, you can check out the FREE Bonus in the beginning of this book….;-)

Email services like AWeber and Mailchimp help you collect the email addresses and allow you to set up auto responders, e.g. welcome and follow up messages.

You will also use them for your newsletters.

If you don't have a website yet, Book #1 in this series will walk you through it Step-by-Step.

Please be aware, that landing page features are only available on self hosted sites like Wordpress ORG - not free blog platforms like Wordpress.COM, Blogger Weebly etc.

This link will give you an amazing deal on the Top rated hosting service and from here you can easily start your site

SassyZenGirl.com/Web-Hosting

Sponsors & Brand Deals

Brand Deals have greatly increased on social media and are expected to grow even bigger in the coming years.

A "brand deal" is a sponsorship deal between a merchant/company and a creator/social media influencer who gets paid to market products to their large audience.

It's different from affiliate marketing where you get a commission every time you generate a sale.

With sponsorships you are paid a fee and/or receive freebies in return for an online review where you introduce the product to your audience.

Obviously, you should only recommend products you can fully stand behind or your credibility and brand will suffer, but once you have a good basic following, brand deals will be a nice way to monetize your social media presence.

There are several platforms to connect companies and influencers and once you have a certain following, companies will also contact you directly.

Here are some of the most widely used options:

Famebit
Famebit used to be only for Youtube, but recently added several other Social Networks.

To join, you need a minimum of 5000 subscribers/followers on one of your accounts, and you can only add one account per platform.

Other companies like **Grapevinelogic** let you start at 1000 and here are a few more options:

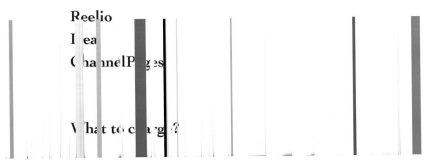

Reelio
Izea
ChannelPages

What to charge?

Knowing what to charge is often a big challenge when you first pitch to brands. Fortunately, there is a widely recognized free tool that can crunch the numbers for you:

Social Blue Book

You can choose a platform - Youtube, Instagram, Facebook, Twitter or Blogger - and authorize the site to access your stats.

Based on those stats - number of followers, number of comments per post, likes, shares etc - Social Blue Book will generate an appropriate pay range for a sponsored post, photo, video, etc.

It even has a feature to write the proposal *for* you, including production costs (for video), agent fees etc.

Advertisers have access to this tool as well, so pitching a Social Blue Book quote will add credibility.

You will find a video on the Resources page that shows you Social Blue Book's features and how to use them.

Tools & Further Training

(please find direct links on the Resources Page)

Scheduling & Management Tools

These tools will be your best friend and help prevent overwhelm and burn out. You can schedule and bulk submit your posts in advance and pick the most effective times when your audience is online.

The 4 most widely used tools are:

SproutSocial
PostPlanner
Buffer
Hootsuite

Content Curation

To find the most relevant and trending content for your niche the following free tools can provide insight and keep you abreast of changing trends.

BuzzSumo - lists the most shared posts for each field by day, week, month, year - and by social network

Feedly - news aggregator
See the Feedly video in the Resources section for a demo

Image Tools

Please find the following article on the Resources Page:
23 Tools and Resources to create Images for Social Media

These are some of the most widely used softwares:

Fotor
PicMonkey
Canva *(super easy to use & FREE!)*
Smart MockUps

Interconnecting Social Media Platforms

IFTTT has some great free applets that help fine tune each of your platforms and help interconnect them.

Contest Tools

Wishpond
PromoJam
WooBox

Brand Deals

Finding Brand Deals
Famebit
Grapevinelogic
Reelio
Izea
ChannelPages

Writing Proposals
Social Blue Book

Mailing List Management
AWeber
MailChimp

Web Hosting
InMotion - use this link for a 56% Discount:
SassyZenGirl.com/Web-Hosting

Chapter 2 - INSTAGRAM

Overview

Instagram is stunning and awesome!

It started as a simple photo sharing app in 2010, but quickly evolved into one of the most powerful marketing platforms on the internet.

The main focus is still stunning visuals, but no longer just photos shared between friends. Rather elaborate designs with amazing images, inspirational quotes, short videos and promotions.

More than 600 Million people are now active users of Instagram, and its rapid rise inspired Facebook to buy the platform in 2012 for a whopping 1 Billion Dollars!

Should you include Instagram in your marketing strategy?

Well, that depends….

Do you have a topic/brand that lends itself to beautiful visuals? A product that you would like to feature in all its beauty? Do you love photography and anything visual?

If yes, then you should definitely consider including Instagram in your social media portfolio.

Brands connected to travel, food, clothing, health, luxury and beauty do especially well. But even the entrepreneurial magazine **Foundr** flourished on Instagram and built a 6 figure following in only 7 months!

Inspirational themes so too all, well. Beautiful images with quotes are great at evoking emotion and creating viral content

If you love beauty and love communicating through stunning visuals rather than just written text - Instagram will probably become one of your favorite platforms - it certainly did for me!

Your overall Marketing Strategy

The same marketing principles apply as for all other platforms: find you brand, your style, your theme and have a clear audience in mind. We covered this in-depth in the first chapter of this book.

Same applies to researching content with that specific audience in mind, rather than blindly posting whatever you think might work.

Develop a clear strategy of what you want to achieve with Instagram. How does it fit into your overall business plan? And into your overall social media strategy?

Spend some time on this step, because it will lay the groundwork for long term Instagram success.

Once you are clear on all the above, you can start creating a profile and your first batch of posts.....

This is the Resources page for all Instagram links and videos:

SassyZenGirl.com/Instagram-Resources

Your Profile

Just like the About page on your website, your Instagram profile is an important piece of advertising and sets the tone for your brand.

It should be fun, attractive and engaging. Someone you would want to hang out with, because in a way your followers will....

Unlike most other social networks, you only get one clickable link - and *only* in the profile, not the post caption - so quite limiting at first sight.

You need to be very clear about what your goal is with this one link and what Call-to-Action (CTA) you want to employ:

- Check out your website
- Sign up to your mailing list *(#10 in Chapter 1...)*
- Access a discount code
- Sell a Product

User Name & Description

Make your user name unique and easy to remember. If you have a brand or blog name, use that.

A nice engaging photo of yourself - or your logo if it's a business - and a warm, engaging bio. Not too long, around 150 characters.

For the link, you can use either your website - or a landing page connected to your website where you offer a free product in return for an email address, or sell a product or service.

A separate landing page allows you to track how many visitors you generate from Instagram vs. other traffic sources, which will be helpful in your analysis.

In that case, use an easy to remember url like:

Yourawesomewebsite.com/STARTHERE or */BIO*

since people will occasionally have to retype it when you suggest that page in post captions, or embed it on an image that might get shared.

Emojis are great and lighten things up. They can also help highlight certain parts of your text like a link or call-to-action. Hands signals work especially well for this.

Once you have completed your profile, you are ready to start creating your first batch of posts…

Your Posts

Instagram allows posting *only* from your mobile phone. Since typing longer captions on mobile can be rather tedious, I will include a few strategies to make the process a little easier.

Consistency

As with all social media platforms, consistency is key!

Throwing out a few posts and then nothing for several days or even weeks will not grow you an audience.

At a minimum, try to do 1-2 post per day and spread them out. Never do several posts at once. It will seem spammy and people might start unfollowing you.

Scheduling

To streamline the scheduling process you can use a tool like **Crowdfire** to schedule a batch of posts in advance. Saves a lot of time and this particular app also provides a lot of feedback to help you grow further.

More on scheduling apps in the **Tools & Training section**.

Content

Whatever you post, it should be visually stunning and original. Don't ever use stock photos.

Content that stirs emotions and engagement. Think about your specific audience. What moves them? What would make them excited enough to follow you and see more of every day?

For inspiration, check out profile that are ila to yours - but with the larger audence

What post have the most engagement? Comments, likes, etc.

Let that inspire you to find your own unique way - one that is easily recognizable after a while.

If you are a good photographer, your photos alone will attract followers. Still, try to be specific and niche down, so your account is not just another of the millions of photographer profiles that hope to be "discovered".

Have a unique take, a specific look, style, topic.

Always include your name/brand or website at the bottom. This has several benefits:

- it protects your copyright

- people can easily find your Instagram profile or website, even if they found your post somewhere else

- it promotes your brand when people start sharing your posts.

You can either use your handle (@yourname), website, or a unique url to a landing page (see above).

Always analyze what specific emotion a picture evokes and use that insight when adding text or captions.

Breathtaking photos combined with an inspiring quote do really well and have a strong viral effect. Again, match the emotion of each.

WordSwag is a great mobile app to create photo quotes for Instagram right on your phone.

Don't limit yourself to just photos though. I found that engagement is often much higher with short video clips - especially in travel. It takes people to the location, rather than just an impression, and the more you can engage people, the more they will love to follow you.

As for **Live Video** - please be aware that live videos are deleted immediately afterwards. That's why it's important to schedule them at the same time each day, otherwise, most followers will miss them.
Or - you can post a photo in story announcing the time of your next live video a reminder.

Caption

Add a location. Ideally a well known location to get more visibility. Why? Because anytime someone searches for pictures in that location, they can see your picture -> additional exposure.

You can also use the location field to insert a clickable url by adding a "new fictional location". Given how limited the options for link placement are on Instagram, this is a nifty little trick.

Adding a nice story in your caption is a great way to stand out and engage visitors with your profile. Instagram is more about tapping into people's emotions. To awe and inspire them, rather than delivering dry information.

Write at least a few paragraphs of valuable, engaging content. You are allowed up to 2,200 characters - that's a lot! Longer captions tend to attract much higher engagement, so don't waste that opportunity.

Make it interesting and unique. People love stories, and following you is then no longer just looking at pretty pictures, but sharing an experience - and who doesn't love that….

Only the first 3 lines will show in the user's feed, so make them catchy enough that people will click for more.

Unfortunately, Instagram does not allow line breaks. - Or so it seems…..

Actually, an easy way to get a line break is to press the "123" key - yep, that's right. Once you do, the return key appears on the right - not really intuitive…

You can also type out the whole text on the notes app of your computer, sync it with the notes app on your mobile device and then copy from there. So much easier than typing with 2 fingers on your phone, especially for longer texts…..

Instagram Stories

Instagram Stories is a new addition and pretty much a copy of Snapchat. It can be a great way to engage with your viewers and you will find a

en *video of Instagram stories on the Resources page*

m is

Using Emojis will make your captions more fun and engaging. Hand signals (pointed fingers/high fives) are great for highlighting a CTA *"click on the link in our bio now to get started"*.

CTAs
Include a CTA (= Call-to-Action) under every post. This could be:

tag your friends
double tab if you agree
click on the link in my bio
share with your friends

And so on.

Also, ask questions and invite feedback. Posts with questions always have a much higher engagement rate.

View every post as an opportunity for your audience to engage with you. The more you do, the faster your following will grow.

A call-to-action in this case does NOT mean:

click on all my links

buy my stuff
recommend me to everyone you know

Every once in a while you can - and should - include those as well, but sparingly. Following you should be fun, not a pitch-fest.

If you are posting an inspirational quote, you could say:

tag someone that inspires you
tag someone who needs to hear this
double tap if you agree and tag a friends who needs to see this

It's important to understand that the only way people can share posts on Instagram is by tagging other users in the comments.

They can share your Instagram posts on Facebook, Twitter and other platforms, but on Instagram itself there is no actual sharing function.

In closing, your goal with each post should be to bring joy and beauty to your followers while also getting them to:

* Share with their friends

* Share their own experiences in the comments
* Find our more about you, your blog, or your company

Schedule

Consistency is key and the most successful Instagrammers post a lot. It depends on your niche - and of course, your free time - so start with a few, 1-3 per day, and see what works for both you and your audience.

There is a correlation between number of daily posts and number of followers, but it is far better to do less per day and do it consistently, than doing 10 in one day and then nothing for several days.

Always be sure to spread your posts over the day. Don't ever post them all at once.

To streamline the process, you can create a pipeline of posts and then automate the scheduling.

Iconosquare and **Crowdflare** can be used for that purpose and even help you pin point the best times to post based on your audience's behavior.

Your Hashtags

No one will find your content, unless you use hashtags = those phrases and words with the # before them.

How to find good hashtags?

Two ways:

1) see what others in your niche are using and compile a long list of potential hashtags for different post types. By analyzing other profiles you can also see which hashtags have the highest engagement (like shares comments)

2) Research: Type a general term from your niche into the search bar. Instagram will show you a number of related hashtags with the amount of posts for each. This will help you pick hashtags that are popular, but not too broad. You want to stay under 100,000, otherwise, your posts can easily get lost in the mass.

Make a list and save it in the notes app on your phone. That way you won't have to type it out every time and can just copy and paste.

For each post, try to use the full 30 hashtags that Instagram allows to spread your net as wide as possible.

However, do NOT put your hashtags in the caption. Put them in the comments instead. They will be just as effective and your posts won't look spammy.

Remember, hashtags are not for people to *see*, but for people to *find* you.

The caption area should look nice and clean. Inviting, not crowded with spammy looking hashtags.

Strategies to Grow your Following

#1 - Find the top influencers in your niche and start **following their followers**. Chances are, they will follow you back, and if you post regularly and provide awesome content, you will quickly build a following.

The point here is to find people who are already interested in what you have to offer. If they follow similar content, chances are they might like yours, too - especially, if yours is even better....;-)

To find top influencers quickly, go once again to the search bar, tap or swipe to tags and type a tag that is relevant in you field,

tap a top post within that hashtag and make sure the account who posted has a lot of followers (definitely more followers than people they are following .

Tap on the number of followers and begin following them one by one.

Keep repeating this with all the top influencers in your niche and with many different hashtags - some may work better than others.

Do a few every day and start building your following consistently.

Instagram has some restrictions regarding how many people you can follow to prevent abuse and spam, so limit yourself to no more than 50 per hour. This may seem a lot, but it really isn't. It only takes a few minutes to tap down the list.

If you do more than 50 per hour Instagram will eventually turn off the Follow function in your account and you can no longer follow anyone....

#2 - Engage

When someone follows you, follow them back - unless it is a spam account.

If someone comments on your photos, always reply and use their handle (@) - unless (once again) it is spam.

Comment and like photos under hashtags you are interested in and also respond to the comments underneath. Tag people you know who might benefit from the photo. Ask questions and invite feedback.

#3 - Shoutouts

"Shoutout" means, another page is recommending your page to their followers. On Instagram, there are two types of Shoutouts:

* S4S (Shoutout for Shoutout) and

* Paid Shoutouts

Lets look at each:

S4S - Free Shoutouts

Find accounts in your niche that are similar to yours - also in the number of followers. Like and comment a few of their photos for a bit while (no spamming pitching our profile) and then contact the owner directly through Instagram DM or an app called Kik.

Ask them if they would be interested in a Shoutout trade.

Paid Shoutouts

For paid shoutouts you want accounts with much higher follower numbers than yours - and high engagement (lots of comments, likes etc) - in other words, an active, thriving account.

Make sure their followers are similar to yours!

You can then either contact the owners directly or use a service like **Shout Cart** to connect you.

The exposure you can get from paid Shoutouts can be tremendous and quickly explode your Instagram account.

Be sure to include a call-to-action, like "follow me" in your Shoutout post - never assume people will just do it, they are far more likely if you ask them to…

#4 - Contests & Giveaways

Contests and giveaways can be a fun way to build a buzz around your account once you have grown a solid following.

It works like this: You find something that's truly valuable to followers of your niche and use it as a give away or prize in a contest.

To enter, participants have to complete 3 steps like:

1) Follow you
2) Like this post and tag 2 friends
3) Sign up to your blog newsletter

= all steps to grow your following.

That's it!

Check out the Resources Page for:

a Social Media Examiner article on
how to plan a successful Instagram Contest

This Hootsuite article with 5 tips and tricks for:
Instagram Giveaway

#5 - Profile Widget on your website

This one is obvious….;-) - you should, of course, have an Instagram widget on your website, ideally one that shows your last few posts.

Instagram Feed is a nice free option for Wordpress sites. You can download it through your plugins page.

Tools & Further Training

please find direct links on the Resources Page

- SassyZenGirl.com/Instagram-Resources -

Scheduling Tools

Check out the Resources page for are more in-depth look at the following 4 apps and their different features:

Later
Publish
Crowdfire
Iconosquare

Another option is Tailwind, which works for both Pinterest and Instagram

Post Creation

WordSwag *to create Picture Quote posts*
Fotor
Canva
Smart MockUps

Promotion

Shoutcart *for shoutouts*

Further Instagram Training

SassyZenGirl.com/Twitter-Instagram-Course

Daily Routine

Try to find a monthly schedule for your post creation.

Certain days when you do all your content research, post creation, tag research, caption writing, scheduling etc.

It's much less overwhelming if you bulk produce a batch of posts per week - or even for the whole month - than having to go through the motions every day.

In addition, try to do the following daily:

) 'cl ov   l s l   llo v rs f t p ir flu ncers in
ou · iel   e #   S r teg es t   3r w your
ol ov ir   or p c   n Jhor th n 5) per hou r).
io th o   a   '   p i flu ic s a d try ma ny
if ere nt   h g t   t n.

2) Comment and like photos under hashtags you are interested in and also the comments underneath them.

Tag people you know who might benefit from the photo. Ask questions and invite feedback.

3) Research influencers in your field (see 1) and make a point of commenting and tagging/liking at least one of their posts daily. No pitching your account, just pure value.

The point is to get on their radar - and be pleasant about it. Eventually, you can contact them, but this is the groundwork to build a relationship. You want to build a wide network of influencers in your niche.

Chapter 3 - PINTEREST

Overview

Dubbed "the World's Catalogue of Ideas", Pinterest has quickly become the search platform of choice for many looking for ideas and inspiration.

The platform has also quickly grown into a premier online market place through the 2015 introduction of "Buyable Pins", allowing businesses to sell products right on the platform.

Made publicly available in 2012, Pinterest has rapidly risen to the top of most relevant Social Media platforms, with currently 150,000,000 monthly users.

At its core, Pinterest is a place where people can organize and share online images. Once uploaded, these images become known as "Pins" which can then be placed on themed "Boards".

But that's just the beginning....

For many users, Pinterest has become something of a virtual pin board and rolodex to store and organize ideas for current and upcoming projects.

Here are some examples:

- Brides-to-be replacing bulky wedding planners with Pinterest boards

- People planning to redecorate their house creating a board for each room and then pinning decorating ideas for that space.

- Authors creating Pinterest boards with book cover images or images they find during research for their novels.

- Artists organizing inspiring images for their work

- Cooks keeping online recipe boxes

- DIY-ers bookmarking tutorials

- Gift guides

- Reading lists

- Playlists

- Event Planning

- Giveaways

and so much more…..

Even in the business world, Pinterest has become a valuable tool:

Companies use Pinterest boards for collaborative projects where each employee can post their ideas and results for everyone to see. This is especially useful when participants cannot work at the same location.

The possibilities beyond just posting pretty images are pretty limitless and not surprisingly, Pinterest's use in a enterprise rise in recent years

From the outset, the majority of Pinterest users have been women though the numbers are gradually evening out - currently 70% to 30% women/men.

The industries most widely represented are retail, fashion, food, and travel, though certainly not limited to those.

To be successful on Pinterest, you need stunning visual content, presented gorgeously with thoughtful descriptions.

The bar is very high and only amazing content has a chance of attracting a long term following.

Whether you should include Pinterest in your marketing portfolio depends on how visual your content is and if you can spend the time to create - or hire someone to create it for you.

The rewards can certainly be enormous, due also to the fact, that Google's algorithm *loves* Pinterest and naturally ranks boards and pages high -> more organic traffic from new customers, certainly much easier than ranking any new website.

Now lets have a look at how Pinterest works and how you can grow a following…..

Your Profile

As always, a good marketing campaign starts with a compelling profile.

Be sure to start with a (free) business account, rather than a personal profile. That way you will have access to a lot more features, including analytics and selling products with "Buyable Pins".

You can add a profile picture or a logo (if you are a business), and enter a brief description of up to 200 characters.

You can add your website as a clickable can choose a name which will also tell you Pinterest

nt rest.com/YourUserName

Include a keyword or two in your description and even your user name, if possible. If you are a photographer, then "photography" or "photos" could be a keyword, similar with other businesses.

Confirm Your Website

It is important to "confirm" your website. Once you do, your profile picture will show on pins that people saved from your site, and you will gain access to Pinterest Analytics.

Please find instructions for confirming your website on the Resources Page

SassyZenGirl.com/Pinterest-Resources

Set up Rich Pins

Rich pins include extra information right on the pin itself. There are 6 different types:

App Pins - include an install button, so pinners can download your app without ever leaving Pinterest.

Movie Pins - include ratings, cast members and reviews

Recipe Pins - include ingredients, cooking times, and serving info

Article Pins - include headlines, author and a brief description

Product Pins - include real time pricing, availability and where to buy. Also price drop notifications

Place Pins - include a map, address, and phone number

The Resources Page features instructions on How to set up Rich pins in your account

Sell on Pinterest

In 2015, Pinterest added "Buyable Pins", allowing businesses to sell products directly on Pinterest via Shopify or Demandware.

Buyers can purchase through an installed app and pay via apple pay or credit card. Pinterest does not charge a fee.

See the Resource Page for Requirements to set up Buyable Pins

Connect your Twitter and Facebook accounts

You should also connect your other social media accounts - currently available are Facebook, Twitter and Google+.

This allows you to tweet your pins and have them show in the timeline of your Facebook followers and friends.

You can also find and connect with your Twitter and Facebook friends on Pinterest.

Your Pins & Boards

Pinterest shares content via "Pins" - basically images with a description. Pins can be organized on "Boards" by topic, and you can also invite others to post to your boards.

You will, however, not share just your own content, but also frequently "re-pin" content from other users. Ideally, it should be a mix of both, not just pure self promotion.

How to find content to re-pin?

You can start with your home feed, look at specific categories and hot trends - or simply enter a keyword in the search bar and browse through the results.

PINS

Use ONLY high quality photos! If you don't, you might as well not pin at all.

In general, tall, vertical images work better than horizontal, because they take up a lot more space -> are more visible.

It's important to have an interesting, keyword rich description. Keywords - so people can find your pins in searches.

Don't include hashtags. It confuses the algorithm and doesn't help people to find you like on Twitter or Instagram.

Images

As for images, Curalate did a widely publicized study featured on **Wired.com** and researched millions of Pinterest images to find the commonalities that make some go viral and others not.

These are the criteria Curalate found to be the common denominators of the most viral Pinterest Images:

- No human faces
- Little Background
- Multiple colors

- Lots of red
- Moderate light and color
- Portrait style

The first point is especially interesting and points towards something very essential to this platform: Pinterest is more about objects/things, while Facebook, for example, is more about people.

Obviously, you can't always incorporate all those aspects, but if you use even a few, chances of images turning viral are a lot higher.

To see which picture actually won - the "perfect" Pinterest image - *go to the Resources Page.*

Consistency

It's important to regularly update your content. One technique to mix this up and automate the process is "looping".

Looping refers to picking up pins from the bottom of the board and repinning them to the top. This makes only sense, of course, with large boards. Otherwise, content would feel repetitive, but with 50 or more high quality pins, it is certainly a technique to keep a board active and engaged.

An easy way to set up looping is a tool named **Board Booster** - one of the two main management tools for Pinterest.

BOARDS

Boards are collections of pins under a specific topic. For example, if your main business/topic is travel, you could create boards for each country, and also travel apps, packing tips etc.

The most successful Pinterest users have very niched down boards - and LOTs of them. In other words, not as generic as I describe above, but rather something more specific like "Beach Hotels", "once-in-a-lifetime road trips" or similar.

Another example would be a home design board split into separate boards for each room. Or a "Dessert" board split into "Pies & Cakes", "Cookies", "Ice Cream" etc

Why?

Because the more niched down, the easier it is to rank, e.g. to be found by people through searches. There is less competition and those that find you are much more *targeted* and therefore more likely to follow and re-pin.

Just like with Pins, include keywords in your Board names and descriptions.

A great way to make your boards stand out is a board widget. *More info on the Resources Page*

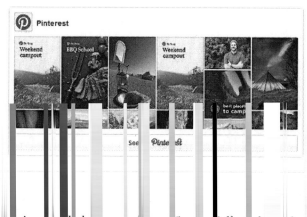

Keep in mind that people prefer to follow boards that are specific to their interests, rather than your entire page. So take great care to make each of your boards a unique and special experience - rather than one grand page with lots of "sub" boards.

Strategies to Grow Your Following

Before we go into specific strategies to grow your Pinterest following, lets first understand how the Pinterest algorithm works.

In 2014, Pinterest launched its new *Smart Feed*, replacing the chronological listing of pins.

Much like Facebook, reaching the top is no longer about when you posted, but whether your pins meet certain quality criteria.

Please check the Resource Page for an article that goes more in-depth on the topic

but these are the main factors:

- **Pin Quality** - high-quality images with substance

- **Source Quality** - share pins from high quality websites and boards, not just your own (esp. when you are brand new)

- **Pinterest Rating** - high quality relevant images with minimal text and no borders - and a well thought-out pin descriptions

As we already saw in the previous chapter, Pinterest is more about things, whereas Facebook is more about people. That's why images without faces are re-pinned significantly more often.

It's important to understand what Pinterest is about and what people are responding to on this particular platform.

I recommend spending some time browsing through the top accounts in your niche and get a sense of what content you need to develop to thrive here.

Pinterest is very different in character from all other social networks u a ring y u tre el dou expos e w e d n r g .

Googl also 'l ves' P n r st nd r r ing a in eres Board vill e l t a ie t a rank n a new w bsit (sim il to Y u u e n th e rd).

Which brings me to the other important ranking factor: SEO - which we'll cover in #6.

Ranking is particularly important with Pinterest, because unlike Twitter or Facebook, your Pins never grow "old".

Content isn't posted chronologically and can instead remain at the top of search results for years to come. Proper optimization is therefore really important.

Now lets dive in and look at 10 effective ways to grow your Pinterest following:

#1 - Follow Others

As with most social media platforms, following others should be your first step.

Pick people in your niche with similar audiences. To find them, put a relevant term or phrase in the search bar and start following the boards that show up.

Follow about 100 per day and wait a few days. Then check who followed you and unfollow the ones that didn't.

Following a number of like-minded people will also show you what visual content is popular in your niche. And it gives you the chance to network (always important on Social Media) and easily find content to re-pin.

Mentioning others in your comments or descriptions, recommending their services, posts or pins or complimenting them, can help start a conversation and most likely they will follow you back.

#2 - Comment on Popular Pins

Another common strategy for pretty much all Social Media. Again, make it a meaningful, longer comment that shows you have read the description and understand the subject. That way, people reading your form which get interested in your board and start following and re-pinning

Be aware though that will Pinterest too much commenting can considered spamming night get you suspend, so just comment five daily day, but consistently.

#3 - Pin frequently & include popular images

Posting consistently and frequently applies to all social media. With Pinterest, you want to have a good mix of your own images and those you re-pin from other boards.

Re-pinning popular images brings out a great feature called: "Also pinned to….".

This is Pinterest's way of connecting people with similar interests. You can check out their boards, find more good pins to re-pin and follow them.

The more you find and pin images people enjoy, the more Pinterest will recommend you (with this feature) to people who pin the same image -> sending a lot more potential followers your way.

#4 - Contribute to Group Boards

Popular group boards often have a large following. If you get invited to pin there, this can turn into a quick and effective way to attract a lot of followers.

Find popular group boards in your niche and form a relationship with the owner. Comment, re-pin etc.   -

then ask to become a contributor. You can find related group boards on **PinGroupie**.com.

Make sure it is an active board with lots of re-pins. Just a high follower number doesn't mean it is a good board to contribute to. You want to see a lot of re-pins and comments per pin.

You can also start your own Group Board and invite others to join in.

#5 - Invite others to Post to your Boards

Create a Board Widget for your most popular boards and invite people to post to it.

This serves two purposes:

1) Contributors will most likely see a lot of your pins = more exposure

2) Your board will show on their page as well > exposure to their audience

As an example, you could ask your followers to post photos of how they interact with your product or service, if that's applicable.

GAP has a board called Styld.by that allows fashion bloggers and clothing aficionados to show off how they wear GAP. Starbucks has a board dedicated to white-cup art and there are many more examples.

People love to participate and it helps grow awareness for your brand.

#6 SEO - Optimizing your Boards and Pins for Searches

Pinterest SEO is a lot less complex than SEO for your website. It's mostly about keyword research and optimizing your Boards and Pins with those keywords.

If SEO is completely new to you, please check out **Book #3** in this series as it is a rather complex topic, but an important corner stone for any website owner and internet marketer.

Keyword Research:

You can use the Google Keyword Planner to get ideas, especially if you also want to rank in Google.

For Pinterest ranking, you can simply enter a keyword or search phrase into the search bar and see what suggestions pop up.

Those are keywords that other users have frequently searched for, that are popular:

Try a few that are relevant to your topic and see what boards and pages come up. Do they have a lot of followers? Lots of re-pins and comments? If yes, then you found yourself a popular keyword.

As important - are they using the exact same phrase in the title and descriptions? If not you have a much better chance of ranking.

It's best to niche down as much as possible with "Long Tail Keywords", meaning phrases longer than 3 words. Those are much more specific and have less

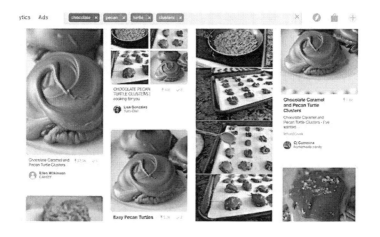

competition -> therefore, a higher chance for you to show at the top.

"Chocolate cookie recipes for Vegans" would be a Long Tail Keyword vs. Just "Chocolate Cookies"

Optimizing your Pins and Boards:
Once you have found a good keyword to target, you need to mention it in the pin/board title and description. Not stuff it, just use it naturally.

A more in-depth look at Pinterest optimization can be found on the Resources Page

#7 - Run a Contest

Running a contest is another effective strategy for most Social Media platforms and very much so for Pinterest.

This is one classic way to set it up:

To enter, participants need to complete the following 3 tasks (or similar):

1) Follow us 2) Repin this image 3) Pin your favorite_____ and include #specialhashtag in your caption.

Ask pinners to create a board with their ideas and use the contest hashtag.

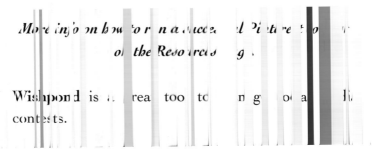

Wishpond is a great tool to manage your contests.

Be sure to read the Pinterest Contest Guidelines. They have some specific rules for contests and you don't want to get suspended for violating them unknowingly.

#8 - Promoted Pins

"Promoted Pins" are Pinterest's version of ads. They allow for specific targeting of both customer interests and keywords.

A nice feature is that you only pay for the first click. So if person A clicks on your promoted pin and re-pins it, you will not pay for anyone repinning what A posted. You only pay for A's re-pin.

Jeff Sieh who currently runs Social Media Examiners' Pinterest campaigns recommends starting with at least $1 per day and has seen good results with $5 per day. Of course, it also depends on your field and proper targeting, but as a ball park number.

#9 - Delete Low Engagement Pins
This is important for Pinterest's algorithm which favors high engagement, viral boards. You want to keep the ratio of active, thriving pins high and remove all those that don't perform well.

Board Booster is once again a great tool to help with this strategy painlessly and quickly.

#10 - Promote on your Website and Social Media

As always, cross promote your Pinterest page on all your other Social Media platforms and your website.

You can use your pins in your posts, place a **Pinterest widget** in the side bar - ideally a profile widget that shows your recent pins - and install a **Pin it button** (Wordpress plugin) to make it easy for people to re-pin right from your page.

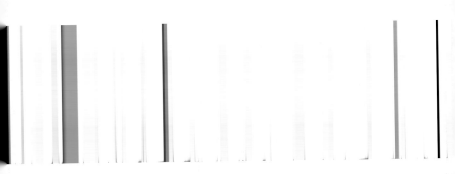

Tools & Further Training

please find direct links on the Resources Page

- SassyZenGirl.com/Pinterest-Resources -

Pin Creation
Pic Monkey
Canva
Smart MockUps

Management & Scheduling
Tailwind (also for Instagram)
Board Booster
Both are great management tools, specifically tailored to Pinterest though Tailwind can also be used for Instagram.
They both feature scheduling capabilities (HUGE time saver), analytics, best time to post and some of the features mentioned in the prior chapters.

Further Training
Pinterest Blogs to Follow:
ManlyPinterestTips.com
MCNGMarketing.com
COURSE - Pinterest For Profits

Daily Routine

- Find 100 new people in your niche to follow.

- Comment on a few popular pins

- Find 20 images to re-pin to *each* of your boards

- Browse through popular boards in your niche, comment, follow users and re-pin appropriate images.

- Be active in Group Boards you would like to be

Chapter 4 - TWITTER

Overview

In 2016, Twitter began to transition from a mere social network to a news platform. In the words of CEO Jack Dorsey in a memo to his employees:

"Twitter is what's happening, and what everyone is talking about (literally!). News and talk. **We're the people's news network.**

People choose us for news because we're the fastest. Fastest to get news, and fastest to share news with the whole world. Now let's strive to be the first. The first place people check to see what's happening...and the first place to break what's happening. In the moment, LIVE, or a fast recap of what we know so far...what matters."

This trend is expected to continue with additional focus on video.

In particular, trending videos, live stream, and broadcast partnerships.

Lets dive in…..

Your Profile

Your profile is once again the first important part of your marketing strategy. Most people will look there first before following you, so be sure to make a powerful pitch.

Profile Photo

Using a photo of your face seems to be most effective and instills trust. Twitter is the ultimate networking platform and people want to see who they are talking to.

Bio

You have 160 characters to introduce yourself. Use a mix of quirky, interesting bio and benefits to your followers.

There are some great examples of Twitter bios on the Resources page to get your creative juices flowing…;-)

SassyZenGirl.com/Twitter-Resources

Pinned Tweet

A pinned tweet allows you to add to your bio. Or you can use it to send visitors to a landing page for a product or email sign up.

Twitter Cards

Twitter Cards installed on your website will make your posts look more appealing and compact when sharing on Twitter.

If you have a Wordpress site, you can use the free Yoast SEO plugin to set up that feature. Just go to the social settings and enable *"Add Twitter card meta data"*.

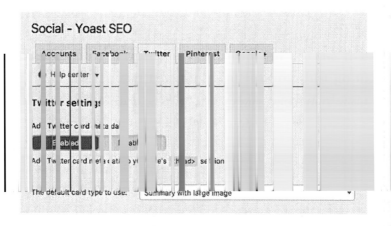

The Resources page has a more in-depth
Twitter Card Guide

Your Tweets

Tweets can have a maximum of 140 characters. If you add a photo, video or poll, that amount decreases by 24 characters, but you can add up to 4 photos.

Sharing a link will take off 23 characters and you need to use a link shortener like bit.ly to make urls sizable for Twitter.

Hashtags
Add a small number of hashtags (2-4), so that others with the same interests can find you, but don't overdo it or your tweets will look spammy.

If you are attending a big event like a sports game or conference, use their official hashtag, so that everyone following the event can see your posts.

What to Tweet?

Try to spread your Tweets among the following 4 categories, so that you are not just posting your own content:

- Internal (your blog posts etc.)
- External (outside posts and articles)
- Inspirational Quotes (very popular with lots of Re-tweets)
- Promotional (recommending your services, products, website etc.)

Tweet Types with high engagement:

The following Tweet types tend to be most successful and encourage a lot of engagement:

- Visual: Photo or Video

- Ask a Question

- Ask an Opinion

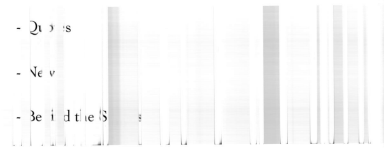

- Qu y s

- Ne v

- Be i d the S s

- Live Events and other real time reporting

- Daily Deals

- Interviews - **see more here**

- Short Memes like "Yes we can", "Just do it", "No Fear"

- Tips

- Tweets with links

Where applicable, include a call-to-action, including asking for retweets. You will be surprised how much more engagement you can get by simply asking.

Tweet Automation

Social Sprout and **Post Planner** can be used to schedule Tweets in advance. Plus, Twitter has its own free platform - **Tweetdeck**

Keep in mind though that Twitter is mostly a news/ live/in the moment network, so pre scheduling all your Tweets is not a good idea. If you want to generate an active following, you have to be engaged and busy on a regular basis and respond to trends and news quickly.
More so than on any other platform.

Strategies to Grow your Following

Growing a following on Twitter is all about engagement and frequency. Actively interacting with other users in your field, participating in conversations, retweeting - and most of all: Tweeting a LOT!

The more engaged you are on a daily basis, the quicker your following will grow.

How often should you tweet?

The more often, the better! There is really no limit here.

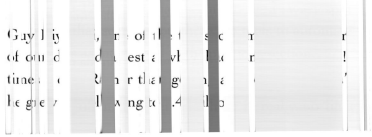

Posting 10-12 times a day seems to be a sweet spot and while that seems a lot, there are tools to automate the process as mentioned in the previous section.

For Twitter, high frequency is one of the main ingredients for rapid growth.

Follow others

The first step to building a following on most social networks is once again: follow others in your field. About 30% of them will follow you back, and it allows Twitter to better understand your brand and niche, so they can suggest your page to other users.

The key is, of course, to follow users that would actually be interested in your content and not just anybody.

How do you find them?

1) Find the top influencers in your field, those with thousands of followers and follow them. If their audience is similar to yours, start following their followers and network with them.

2) Find relevant hashtags (those words with # before them) and look at who is actively participating in the discussion. Again, follow them and network.

These tools can help you automate the process:

Twellow
WeFollow (for finding influencers)
Tweepi (follow someone else's followers, incl. Influencers of your choice - see point 1)
ManageFlitter (bio searches and for keeping an eye on your followers)

Follow around 100-150 people a day and mostly active people, not businesses. Check once a week who hasn't followed you back and unfollow them.

TwitNerd can automate this function for you.

It's important to keep a ratio of at least 1:1 ratio following : followers. If you follow way more people than follow you, your page comes across a spammy (or desp r …) o it's in rtan to gu weed out the c e na c n t f l ou ck

Engage

Following alone is, of course, not enough. Next, you need to engage. Here are 10 ways to do just that:

#1 - Twitter Etiquette. Always follow back, unless it's a spam account. Thank people for retweets and mentions and return the favor. Respond to comments etc.

In other words, engage with the people who engage with you. Not only is it polite, but it also keeps their enthusiasm going to share your content.

#2 - Start interacting with large Twitter accounts, those with thousands of followers. Try to get on their radar. Keep in mind, one retweet from them to their large following can give you a LOT of exposure.

- Keep retweeting their posts and be sure to include their handle (@) so they are aware

- Respond to their Tweets. This allows you to engage with a large audience, plus, your response tweet is attached to theirs for everyone to see.

- Mention them in a Tweet once in a while

- Use **BuzzSumo** to find the top tweeted articles in your fields. Read them and find an angle or additional area that you could improve. Write an article on that, mention the influencer in the article and let them know.

Do this consistently with many different influencers. If even one retweets you, it can mean hundreds of thousands of views and some of them will certainly start following you.

#3 - Search hashtags in your field and jump into the conversation.

NO pitching whatsoever! - Add value, answer questions and have something interesting - non self-serving - to say. This is about networking. Follow other members of the discussion and some will follow you back.

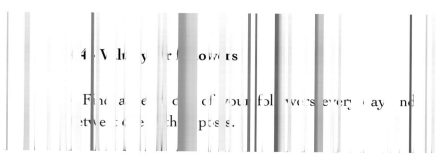

- Thank those who regularly retweet and comment. Favorite one of their tweets to show that you are noticing them.

- Follow those who retweet or favorite your tweets, especially when they take the time to read an article you wrote and left a comment.

#5 - Use Twitter Lists

When you add people to a Twitter list, it is a compliment and lets them know that you find their content valuable. They are likely to return the favor and also follow you back.

A way to automate this process it **IFTTT**. You can set certain hashtags and whenever someone tweets with that hashtag, they get automatically added to your list.

#6 - Use Storify

If you don't know Storify, there is a video on the Resources Page to give you a quick introduction.

Storify allows you to create "stories" by piecing together posts from various social media platforms, in particular Twitter, Instagram and Youtube.

More importantly, it automatically tweets at everybody mentioned in your story and they will want to read what you said. Chances are a number of them will reply, retweet and follow you back.

A retweet will expose you to their audience and if the account is large that one retweet can generate a lot of followers with just one story.

#7 - Participate in Twitter Chats

A great chance to network, share your expertise and get noticed. Again no pitching, just value and networking.

#8 - Discover and Retweet

The "Discover" tab shows the top trend... d   it   i...
your fiel Find a fe post s t a yo ag   it   ...n...
retweet en . Don' forg t to ne   or   ... na...
author.

#9 - Tweet other Blogs

In a similar vein, find relevant blog posts and tweet them. Be sure to include the author's Twitter handle and the blog's Twitter account, so they know.

A great tool for finding such content and keep track of your favorite blogs and Youtube channels is **Feedly**.

If you don't know Feedly, there is a Demo Video on the Resources Page

#10 - Click-to-Tweet plugin

Click-to-Tweet is a free Wordpress plugin that allows you to embed a quote from your article as a clickable button into the text. Readers are encouraged to tweet that quote by clicking "Click to Tweet".

Tweetable quotes are a simple and elegant way to bring more traffic from Twitter http://ctt.ec/n6oH1+ @nickchurick

⟶ CLICK TO TWEET

Promote everywhere

You should promote your Twitter handle everywhere:

- Have a Twitter widget on your blog

- List your Twitter account on your other social media platforms

- Use the Click-to-Tweet plugin

- Embed your Twitter handle on graphics, pictures, videos, and the covers of your other social media platforms

- Add your Twitter handle to your business cards and email signature

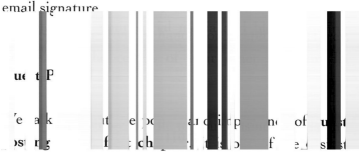

ways to grow your social media and blog following quickly!

Guest posts can continue to drive new followers to your social networks, long past their original posting date, because they will keep showing in Google's search results for years to come.

__Get a special discount on the Top Guest Blogging Course on the Resources Page__

Tools & Further Training

(please find direct links on the Resources Page)

SCHEDULING TOOLS

Tweetdeck *(free - Twitter only)*
SproutSocial
PostPlanner
Buffer
Hootsuite

CONTENT CURATION

TrendsMap - real-time mapping of Twitter trends across the world
Google Trends

Sto
Fee

FO   OWI R ANA E   N

Twi   d
Twellow
WeFollow
Tweepi
ManageFlitter

Daily Routine

- Choose 5-7 big influencers in your field. Pick one for each day of the week and then rotate again. Use **Tweepi** to follow 100-150 of that person's followers. Check twice a week who followed you back and unfollow those who didn't. (**TwitNerd** can help)

- Comment / retweet a few influencer tweets

- Find trending hashtags and Twitter chats in your field and participate in the conversation.

- Use the "Discover" function as well as Feedly and BuzzSumo to find hot content to retweet and comment on.

- Find at least one of your followers every day and retweet one of their posts. Favorite tweets from followers who regularly retweet and comment.

- Create a story on Storify

- Research and schedule your own tweets with Tweetdeck

Chapter 5 - FACEBOOK

Overview

Whatever your brand or business, you need a Facebook Business Page.

Why?

Bec u   a   o   l fa t e r st vide se
soci l   o   l   i ic e er ne mo t o
frie ds   nt   l l ve a ac oo pro l a
t e e   u   o   s ss a es fe an na i
a ra t   a   ar ti ols

For example, you can sell products right from your Facebook page, offer your services - and even

114

integrate scheduling capabilities, so your customers can schedule appointments through your page.

You can showcase your brand with Photo albums, video playlists and company milestones.

You can schedule live events and invite people.

And you can live stream videos from your mobile device straight into your follower's news feed - a new feature that Facebook is heavily promoting.

Facebook Ads have become one of the most powerful marketing tools on the internet with a sophisticated algorithm that lets Facebook fine tune your targeting *for* you.

So not using Facebook and its many amazing features would leave one of the most important internet marketing tools on the table.

Excited?

Then lets begin!

Your Profile

If you don't know how to start a Facebook Business Page, there is a video on the Resources page with a quick demo.

SassyZenGirl.com/Facebook-Resources

Now lets look at all the different marketing features your page offers and how to set them up.

Think of your Facebook Business Page as a glamorous storefront where you can showcase your business with photos, videos, stories, even an actual store or services page, reviews and so much more.

Design it beautifully, as you would with your website. People will decide within just a few seconds whether they will "like" your page. Give them as much reason to say yes, as you can.

Cover & Profile picture

A great tool for creating an engaging Facebook cover is **Fotor.**

Look on the Resource Page for Facebook Cover Photo Best Practices

The cover should be visually appealing and not have too much text. Aside from your brand name, you can add your website url and Twitter or Instagram handle to make it easy for new visitors to find you on other platforms.

As mobile and desktop versions have different cover dimensions, try to keep text mostly in the center, so it won't get cropped.

About

The About area on Facebook business pages has become rather elaborate with many different tabs and sub options. Try to fill them out as completely as you can.

Write an engaging - not too stuffy - description of what you do, offer and stand for, keeping in mind that the first 1-2 sentences will show as a snippet in the right side bar on the main page. That's the first piece of information visitors will see.

Add all your other social media profiles, your website, biography, awards, affiliations etc. in the appropriate tabs and write a compelling "Story".

Additional Features

Next, click on "Settings" in the upper right hand corner. This is where you access most of the business features and tools. Lets have a look:

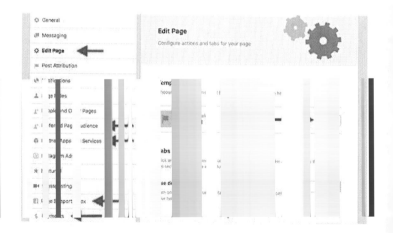

Templates & Tabs

Facebooks offers a number of different Templates suited for:

Shopping - Business - Venues - Politicians - Services Restaurants & Cafes (with a menu feature)

with various call-to-action buttons for the top menu, including "Call me" or "Learn more".

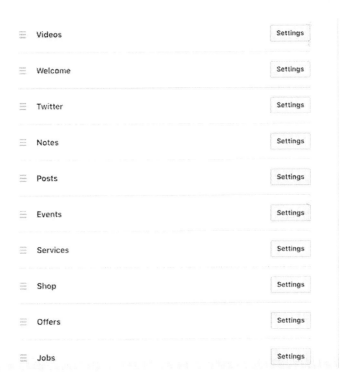

Below that, you can choose which tabs you want to appear in the left side bar.

Of particular interest are:

Services: to list - you guessed it... - your services if applicable

Shop: to sell your products right from your Facebook page. The last feature under settings - "Payments" - allows you to connect with either PayPal or Stripe to receive payment.

Offers: Discounts etc.

Jobs: if your are hiring

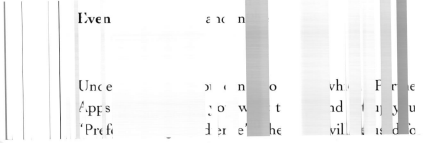

ads and whenever Facebook is suggesting your page to someone new.

The apps can assist you in anything from scheduling appointments to fulfilling orders - all right within your Facebook page!

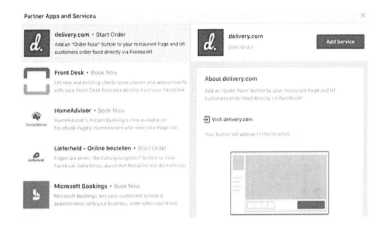

You can also set up a customer service Inbox under "Page Support Inbox".

Photo Albums & Video Playlists

Next, you want to add a number of photos (simply create a few photo posts) and organize them in Photo Albums. This is a great way to visually showcase your business and products.

Also, add a few videos and sort them in playlists.

Milestones

Then you can add a few milestones of your business.
Founding, awards, successes etc.

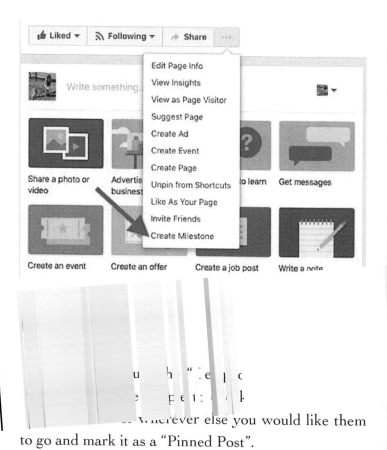

wherever else you would like them to go and mark it as a "Pinned Post".

That's it! - You've now set up an inviting Business page to feature your brand and market your services or products.

Your Posts

As with all social networks, regular posting - at least once a day - is crucial. Not only to keep your followers engaged, but more importantly, to improve your "Reach" within Facebook's algorithm.

What is "Reach"?

Well, did you know that only 16% of your Followers will actually get to see your Posts!

This is something most people are not aware of.

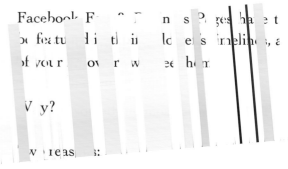

Facebook F   n s ges ha e t
 featu i t i l e s ineli , a
f you o r w e h m

V y?

 reas :

1) It forces users to use Facebook Ads to broaden their reach, even among their own followers.

You can always "boost" a post to your existing followers to make sure they will get to see it. So it's certainly a way to increase Facebook's ad revenue.

That's not all though, in fairness:

2) Facebook is trying to make the newsfeed as user friendly and uncrowded as possible.

With so many people and businesses now having pages, your newsfeed would be completely overcrowded and it would be hard to find the content you actually want to see.

Hence, while your friends' posts still show, pages you follow will have to compete for a spot in your timeline.

It works as follows:

When you post something to your page, it will be seen by only a small number of your followers - maybe 25-100. Depending on their level of engagement (likes, shares, comments) the algorithm will determine your "score" and decide if and how many more of your followers get to see that post.

All the while you are competing against every other page that's posting at that same time and shares the same followers!

The algorithm rewards active pages with engaged audiences and "punishes" those with low engagement - who will then have to pay for Ad Boosts to reach their audience.

While frustrating at times, not an altogether unreasonable idea.

The other factors that determine your reach are:

* A user's previous interactions with your page. Do they like, share, comment a lot - only a little - or not at all. All this determines the likeliness of t[...]
seeing your f[...] posts and you[...]

[illegible distorted text]
u[...] [...] interactions [...]
t[...] [...] in
[...]l [...] back ("I don[...] see this

* When it was posted. The older the post, the lower the score

126

Timing your Posts

Because of this unusual feature, it makes more sense to post during off-peak times to face less competition - the opposite of what you would do on most other social networks.

Posting right before peak times is ideal. You'll have less competition, therefore generate a higher score that will then carry over into peak time -> wider reach.

How often should you post?

Facebook's algorithm favors quality over quantity, so while you should post regularly and at least once a day, quality should always be your #1 priority.

The algorithm is designed to filter out low quality posts and ensure only popular, engaging content gets through to the user.

Your time is better spent creating a few great posts that your followers will love and share, than a lot of low quality junk that might actually earn complaints.

Post Pictures and Videos

Facebook loves pictures and videos and favors them in their algorithm.

Engagement rate is also a lot higher with visual content, in particular video.

That's why it's important to fill your photo and video tabs with appealing content right from the start as visitors often love to browse through them.

Facebook Live is a new feature that allows live broadcasting from your mobile device right into people's news feed.

Facebook's algorithm gives preference to live video over regular ~~posts~~ ~~and~~ ~~marketers~~ ~~focus~~ ~~on~~ ~~video~~

... following and raise your reach score, spend some time on researching the most effective content to share.

If you read **Book #2**, you already know how to do that. In short, these are two ways to get started:

1) Look at the leading influencers in your genre and see what type of content they are posting on a regular basis. What topics are trending. What posts have the most engagement? What do the comments say?

Follow pages that have a similar audience and topics as yours, but far more followers - and very active ones.

2) Use **BuzzSumo** to quickly research the most shared Facebook posts of the day, past week, past month etc. - and choose your topics accordingly.

Try to spread your content over the following 4 areas:

- External content *(Feedly and BuzzSumo can help you find interesting content for your niche)*

- Internal content - *your own blog posts, videos, photos*

- Inspirational Quotes - *always hugely popular and shareable*

- Promotional - *occasionally pitch a product or service*

More on winning post types in the next chapter.

Overall, be fresh, new, interesting - no recycling the same old, same old ...

y ur e ga i l v,   l   r
 ert. t's t   t   p .

u ill kr   e y r   t
n he d re   a k of y ur audience - or not.

Strategies to Grow Your Following

First Steps

Once you have set up your page, these are the next 3 steps to get your first initial followers:

1) Invite all your Facebook friends.

2) Share your Business Page across all your other social media platforms and invite your email list.

3) Add a "Follow" button and a social share bar on your blog or website. I recommend a floating bar that stays with the reader while scrolling down. A good, free one is the Wordpress plugin SumoMe.

Engage

Respond to any user engagement quickly, be it a post comment or message. Facebook measures your response time and factors that into the ranking. There is also a tab at the top right telling visitors how quickly you respond.

Post types that encourage engagement

We already covered the importance of visual content. Now lets look at specific post types that stimulate engagement.

- Ask a question, opinion, feedback, personal experiences etc.

- Fill in the Blank_____: "When I'm a Millionaire, I will _____"

- Include Calls-to-action - "Tag someone you know

- Inspirational quotes do really well and are highly sharable

- Same with Memes - and they are easy to create.

There is a free Meme Generator on the Resources Page

- Polls and votes. You can even let people vote with a *like* or a *share*:

To choose option A -> Like

To choose option B -> Share

The more controversial the topic, the more engagement.

Techniques to widen your exposure

Shoutouts with Tags
Include tags in your posts, especially when working with other organizations/pages or when you try to get the attention of a larger brand or influencer.

When they notice your tag, they might share your post with their followers, giving you great exposure.

Be generous with tags: conferences you are attending, businesses whose articles you are sharing, favorite clients etc.

The more you connect, the faster you will grow.

#Hash it out

Similar to tags, plus they allow you to cross promote over various social media platforms like Twitter and Instagram.

You can also categorize your posts by topic and search hashtags to discover fan conversations you may want to participate in.

Organic Post Targeting

For each post, you can target a specific region among your audience depending on the topic. To do this, simply click on this icon:

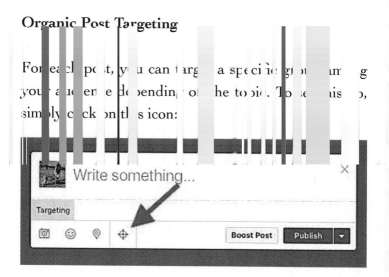

Even within the competitive nature and limited reach of Facebook's algorithm, you can now target those followers that are most likely to be interested in your post.

Participate in the Conversation

Find relevant Facebook and Reddit groups and participate in the conversation. No pitching or self-promo, really try to add something interesting and valuable, help people, share interesting points of view etc.

If people like you or think you are an expert, they will automatically check out your page.

If someone shares a problem or frustration, create a little Youtube video or blog post that answers and helps with that very topic and include it in your answers.

That's different from pitching your business or site! - You are providing help and support where it was actually requested, and that will be much more enticing to people than jamming your page in their face (which could also get you banned).

In other words, become a master networker.

Facebook Ads

The fastest way to grow an audience - and not just on Facebook - are Facebook Ads. They have long overtaken Google Ads in effectiveness and can specifically target an audience based on a number of pre-set demographics, as well as behavior patterns of your website visitors.

How to effectively run Facebook Ad campaigns can be a rather complex topic, but to get you started,

I included a Facebook Ad Guide by master marketer Neil Patel on the Resources Page

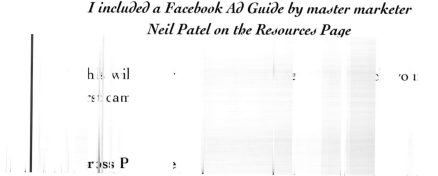

Promote your Facebook page on your other social media platforms and your website. You can install a

profile widget in the side bar that shows your most recent posts or a gallery of your followers.

Also mention your Facebook url on your business card and email signature.

Monitor your Analytics
As with any marketing campaign, keep an eye on your analytics.

This will tell you:

1) the demographics of your audience

2) which posts and post types work well - or not

Keep abreast of those data and adjust where needed. It's another of the many great marketing tools Facebooks offers.

Tools & Further Training

(please find direct links on the Resources Page)

SassyZenGirl.com/Facebook-Resources

Scheduling

Facebook now allows you to schedule - and even backdate - your posts right from within your page.

If you still want a more compact management tool that includes other social networks, these 4 can help you:

SproutSocial
PostPlanner
Buffer
Hootsuite

Cover creator
Fotor
Canva
Pic Monkey

Content Curation
Feedly
Buzzsumo
Meme Generator

THE ULTIMATE FACEBOOK COURSE!

Often referred to as the "Queen of Facebook", and ranked #4 on Forbes' Top Social Media Power Influencer list, Mari Smith was selected by Facebook to partner as the company's leading Small Business and Facebook Marketing expert.

If you are serious about growing your business on social media - and Facebook in particular - this is the course to take!

Direct link on the Resources Page

Daily Routine

- Be active in related Facebook Groups and Reddit threads. Provide help and great info and network with others. This can also lead to collaborations, mutual shoutouts, guest posts - and, of course, sharing of your content.

Networking will be your #1 traffic generator on Facebook - aside from ads!

- Follow other - larger - pages in your niche and start actively commenting, liking, sharing. Once again, NO self-promo or pitching. Be selfless, provide value and support. The point is to get on the r

- Post regularly - at least once a day.

Chapter 6 - YOUTUBE

Overview

Youtube is the #2 most popular website in the world, right after Google and *before* Facebook according to Alexa ranking.

It is unique among social media platforms in that it's not only a social network, but also a search engine.

In fact, it is the 2nd largest search engine right after Google (who *owns* Youtube) - and bigger than Bing, Yahoo and Ask! combined!

Youtube broadcasts about a third of US Multimedia Entertainment, and every second about 50,000 videos are viewed all around the world!

Youtube Ad spending by the top 100 advertisers has increased by 50% in the last year alone and brand deals with Youtube creators have been on a steady rise - a trend that's expected to grow even more in the coming years.

So if you haven't built a Youtube presence for your business or brand yet, it's probably time....

More and more, consumers prefer video as their main source of information. It takes much less effort to watch a video than read a blog post, and many times a "How-to" video is much easier to follow than reading a text with lots of screen shots.

Not having an online video presence at all could mean a loss of potential clients and readers - and missing out on an entirely different way to connect with

For most of us, daily vlogging would be too time intensive, with filming, editing and marketing daily

142

episodes. But even if you just post a new video once a week - or even once a month - you can start seeing a difference in the way you are connecting with your audience - and attract new viewers and subscribers.

It is much easier - and faster - to rank a Youtube video, than an article on a new blog. Ranking high in Google that is.

Why?

Because Youtube's Domain Authority is 100 - the highest possible - while most new websites have values of less than 10 usually.

If the terms "ranking" and "Domain Authority" don't mean anything to you, no worries - those are SEO terms and you can learn the basics of SEO - the parts that every blogger and website owner needs to know - in **the 3ʳᵈ book of this series**.

SEO is also an important success factor for Youtube. In fact, most successful Youtubers agree, by far THE most important factor to get new subscribers and views.

In other words, if you want to be successful on Youtube, you need to know at least the basics of SEO!

Build a Brand, not a Channel

As with any business, social media platform or website, it's important to first focus on clearly defining what your channel is about - specifically.

What is your brand?

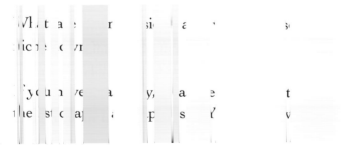

Be very clear about WHO your audience is and WHY they would be watching you. Have a specific person in mind who you talk to when you are on camera. Not a real-life person necessarily, but an avatar that defines your specific audience to a tee.

Your camera appearance will be different when you are "talking" to a specific person, rather than just the general void....;-)

It will also change and fine tune the topics you choose and how you present them. Your style, your brand - what makes you unique.

This part will always be the most important no matter what new venture you start. Get that right and everything else will fall into place much easier.

Value Proposition

Also, clarify what specific value your channel offers to that audience? How do you make their lives easier? Either by solving a problem or frustration, teaching something they need, providing a dose of inspiration - or entertaining them, making them laugh.

Be very clear about WHY someone would want to watch your channel, what they need and what they are looking for.

And most importantly - what is unique about your channel that viewers won't find anywhere else?

Why would viewers want to binge watch a whole playlist in your channel, for example? - happens a lot with successful Youtubers.....

This will obviously evolve over time and won't be "perfect" right away - and it doesn't need to be - but start somewhere and keep an eye on these important questions and where you may need to adjust or change direction.

Focus is power! The more clearly defined you are on the above points, the easier you will progress and attract the "right" people to your channel, the ones that are looking for your specific content.

The biggest mistake you can make is being too general

Also, if you are worried about all the tech stuff, you can hire with a tech savvy high school kid who would love to to make a few extra bucks or find someone of similar interests to partner with (see Chapter 1).

Patience & Persistence

Building a Youtube following takes time and it is a LOT of work!

First, there is all the technical stuff you need to learn: filming, editing, designing thumbnails, marketing, storytelling, presenting in front of a camera and much more.

It can seem overwhelming at first, especially, if all of the above is new to you.

It is definitely by far the most work intensive of all Social Media platforms - and most of all, the one with the steepest learning curve.

So be sure you are up for it and really passionate about creating videos. Otherwise, you might soon get frustrated and give up.

You will need a consistent posting schedule of at least once a week or Youtube might stop promoting you and subscribers could leave as they are expecting regular new content.

It is quite a commitment, especially in the beginning when you are still learning all the technical stuff.

You need a long term mind set.

Learning what is taught here and applying it from the beginning, will give you a good head start. You are going into this adventure with open eyes and a clear understanding of how this works and what you need to do.

If you stay consistent - and keep reviewing and adjusting along the way - you have a great chance of being successful!

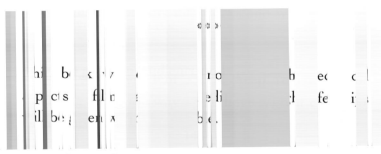

Instead we *will* focus on:

- How to grow an Audience and

- How to make money with Youtube

Where to Start

Youtube provides a lot of helpful tools for creators and I will mention them as we go along.

I also recommend signing up for their free **Creator Academy** and **Creator Community** for support and networking opportunities.

I will occasionally link out to videos from the top training channels on Youtube. They have an abundance of great information, and I encourage you to subscribe and keep improving and learning in the coming months.

To make it easy, I have embedded all videos and resources on the Resources page. Just click on the link below and keep that page open in a separate window, so you can quickly move back and forth:

SassyZenGirl.com/Youtube-Resources

Now lets go Youtube…;-)

Your Channel

The first step in every Youtube career is signing up and customizing a new channel.

You can find a video with how-to instructions on the Resources Page.

Your channel will be connected to either your Google+ profile or a Google Business Page. I recommend the latter, so all your social networks are connected under one brand, rather than you personally.

More importantly, with Google+ your channel name has to be your name, whereas with a business page

o c   c   s   e   n   ı t   ıε   ℩ı
rᶻ ıc

ıe iı ᵶ eᵻ

To access all of Youtube's features, you need to first get your account "verified".

See Resources Page for Video Tutorial

Verification enables the following features:

- *Monetization* - allows you to run ads on your videos
- *Custom Thumbnails* - more on that in the next chapter
- *Video Length* - can be longer than 15 minutes
- *Live Streaming*
- *Copyright disputes*
- *Annotations* - text overlays on your videos, often with links to other videos or your website
- *Branding* - you can add a logo at the lower right hand corner of the screen for all your videos
- *Custom url* - a url using your channel/brand name, rather than a long succession of numbers and letters

http://youtube.com/c/YourBrandName

vs.

https://www.youtube.com/channel/
UCpAKaIIhMSwZoC0GpjhE7qQ

Usually a custom url requires a minimum of 100 subscribers, but if you connect your website, you can start right away.

See Resources Page for Video Tutorial

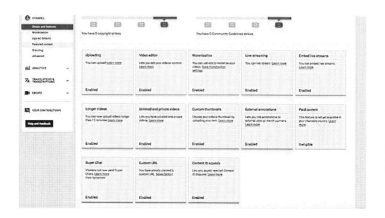

Channel art design

Your channel design will set the tone for your brand and what people can expect. You will add both a profile picture and the cover.

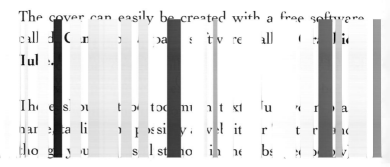

Keep text mostly centered as cover dimensions vary greatly between devices (desktop, mobile etc).

About

Add a compelling bio, something interesting and fun that entices visitors to find out more.

The first 2 lines will show in a pop-up whenever someone hovers over your channel name, so make them catchy enough that people will click for more.

Your About section should make it easy to quickly understand:

- what your channel is about
- how it benefits subscribers
- who your audience is
- your posting schedule

Include a few keywords, e.g. words or phrases relevant to your genre. A photographer would include the words "photo" or "photography" to make it easy for the Youtube and Google bots to understand what your channel is about. This again for ranking/SEO purposes.

Channel Trailer

A channel trailer is a free piece of advertising Youtube includes, and they also use it to promote your channel.

Content should be similar to the about section, ideally 30-60sec in length - short and sweet - and will help viewers decide whether your channel is for them and whether they "like" the presenter.

End with a strong "Call-to-Action (CTA)" to subscribe. As a reminder a "Call to Action" is a little "command" to let your audience know what you want them to do: subscribing, sharing, liking, commenting etc.

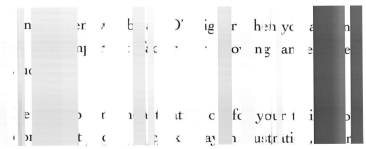

you even had a chance to make your pitch.

Connect your other Platforms

Youtube makes it easy to cross promote with your other social media platforms or website.

Just hover over the cover picture, click "Edit links" and enter the networks you want to show in the upper right hand corner.

You can even add your Amazon store if you are an affiliate.

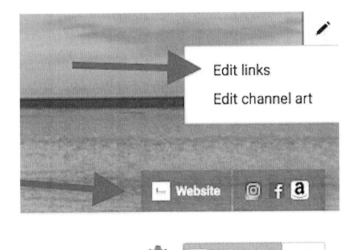

Playlists

Playlists are a great way to keep visitors engaged with your channel.

They also allow you to appear twice in the YouTube search results, and your channel looks a lot more organized to new visitors.

Think of what topics you are covering with your brand and create different playlists for each. Then keep adding videos as you upload them.

You can add one video to several playlists if there is an overlap and you can always change the order of the list.

Don't forget to give each playlist a keyword rich title and description - again for ranking purposes.

Youtube loves playlists, because they increase "Viewer Watch Time"

Your Videos

PRE-PRODUCTION

While we will not cover the technical aspects of film making, there are a number of marketing strategies you can employ in the creation process, that will greatly help you help attract an audience.

First of foremost:

Content Research

Research your video idea BEFORE you get started! - Make sure whatever topic you choose will have an interested audience and ideally a large one.

As a start, I would subscribe to at least 10 successful channels in your genre and watch what content they post and what is doing particularly well.

Really explore what's out there in your field. What types of videos, what topics, what trends. How do they present the info, what techniques do they use.

Spend at least a few days just getting an overview and really immerse yourself in your "scene".

Keyword Research

Remember, SEO is the #1 success strategy in Youtube to attract subscribers and views: People searching for specific content and clicking on one of the top 5 to 10 videos showing in the search results.

How do you rank?

Well, **book 3** will give you a more detailed response to that question, but in Youtube ranking happens most of all through keywords = search terms that people enter to find what they are looking for

More on finding them in the **SEO chapter** of this book.

For the purposes of this section, we want to research what *type* of video shows up when you enter a keyword idea. Are there many, and do they use the same exact phrase? Do they have lots of views and comments?

Mostly big channels with lots of subscribers or medium to new?

What gets people excited and can you create something better?

With social media, the main intention is always to get people to *interact* with your content - to comment and share.

You need to figure out what content in your niche does just that - and why?

Content Types

Tim Schmoyer, one of the top video marketing coaches and himself a successful Youtuber of many years, advises to have a mix of:

- **Discoverable content** for new users who find you through searches and have never heard of you

- **Community content** for your regular viewers who have specific needs and questions that you respond to with your videos

Discoverable content needs to be attention grabbing.

Could be a trending topic that you incorporate into your brand with a catchy headline and thumbnail. Or a viral trend like the recent mannequin or ice bucket challenges.

Be creative...

The 2 most important Marketing Features for any

- Thumbnail

because that's how people find you in the search results.

Title

You need an irresistible title and a thumb nail that stands out and invites to click through.

Your main keyword needs to be in the title, ideally in the front, followed by an emotionally compelling second half ("_____you MUST master in 2017).

The one must have tool for Youtubers - **TubeBuddy** - makes this process a lot easier for both keyword and title research, and I will mention more of its many features throughout this chapter.

Thumbnails

Successful Youtubers spend almost as much time developing awesome thumbnails (= your video cover image) as they spend on the entire production..... That gives you a good sense of how important thumbnails are.

You need to stand out in the search results - make a flash and be easily recognizable as your brand.

See a video on this topic on the Resources page

TubeBuddy makes it super easy to create awesome thumbnails and also stores templates for further use.

See a demo video on the Resources page

Here are a few more tools for thumbnail creation:
Canva
PicMonkey

For free photos you can use:
GraphicStock
FreeImages
Creative commons in **Flickr**

PRODUCTION

Now lets get to the production part.

How to record your computer screen?

For "**How-to**" **videos** a combination of Powerpoint slides and screen recordings works really well - or just screen recordings.

Screenflow is usually the software of choice.

Camtasia is another option.

Outros & Intros

A cool looking Intro and Outro will give your videos a more professional appearance - and they are not expensive to create.

You can try a few Fiverr gigs for often just $5 or use a software called **Outromaker** to create these clips yourself.

Editing Softwares

Check out the videos in the Resources page for:

- a Comparison of Editing Softwares

- On-camera Performance & Body Language

These are the 3 main points:

* Hold eye contact - look directly at the lens, don't let your gaze stray
* Open arms
* Smile and remember there is a human on the other side of the camera. Talk to a person as though they were right in the room. You can even place a picture behind the camera as a reminder.

Please note that "royalty free" does not mean "free" - not necessarily. You often pay a flat fee for a license and can then use that music as often as you like - within - the specific parameters of the license.

Always check that "Commercial Use" is allowed if you plan to monetize your videos with ads or for affiliate reviews.

The license will also specify how the copyright owner wants to be credited. Be sure to follow these instructions to the letter, because copyright infringement is a serious matter and using copyrighted music without proper permission can quickly incur a copyright strike (penalty) on your channel!

A first strike will keep you running, but for 6 months a number of important features will be turned off (custom thumbnails! - longer videos, monetization etc.). So a strike is a big deal.

Should you ever receive one, you can appeal, but best not to ever get one in the first place....

Most channels will occasionally get hit with a copyright *claim* (NOT a strike). This does not have punitive consequences. It simply means that someone claimed copyright and can now collect half or all of your ad revenue.

You can always appeal, but it's a rather frustrating process since the Youtube Copyright team is anything but helpful, keeps people waiting, and then just offers generic replies. Unfortunately, there is no phone support.

Here are a number of sources for royalty free music - both paid and free.

Paid

Audio Blocks
For $99 per year you get unlimited access to a huge selection of tracks and songs. If you produce a lot of videos, this is a great deal

Audio Jungle
per song flat fee

Free

Youtube's Free Music Library
Features both music and sound effects.

InCompetech

CC Mixter
be sure to select "commercial free use"

Josh Woodward
He only asks that you give him credit and spread the word about his music. Mostly vocal music.

Copyrighted Music
To check whether one of your favorite songs can be used in a video, go to:

Creator Studio (within your Channel Dashboard) -> Create -> Music Policies

Most popular songs will be listed there with specific instructions on how they may be used.

POST PRODUCTION

Check out the video on the Resources Page for:
How to upload a new video to your Channel

While your video is uploading you can add your meta data - more on those in the SEO Chapter - and your custom thumbnail.

Once your video has finished uploading, you can add annotations and/or cards.

Annotations

Please note - annotations don't work on mobile.

Cards

Cards are an interesting alternative to annotations - and they do work on mobile. Cards offer some amazing marketing options, so be sure to

Check out the video on Cards on the Resources Page

You have to choose between cards or annotations for each video - you can't use both.

End Screen Cards

End Cards cover the last 20 seconds of your video, so keep that in mind during production.

Check out the video on End Cards

Captions and Transcripts

There are several reasons why adding captions is a good idea:

- Viewers in other countries will have an easier time following you. Even native speakers often prefer captions.

- If a subscriber wants to translate your videos, they will need a caption file.

- If you want to upload your videos to Amazon's Video on Demand (free upload) you will need closed caption. Same for Facebook.

- If helps with ranking/SEO. The more info Youtube has, the more accurately they can rank you - not necessarily higher as is sometimes confused, but more accurately for your specific keyword and genre.

named **rev.com**. You can get captions and transcripts for just $1 per min of footage and they also offer translations at just 10c per word.

So rather than spending an hour or two transcribing manually, this is a great option.

Adding Time Stamps

For longer videos, your viewers will appreciate if you add clickable time stamps in the description.

There is a video on the Resources Page that shows you how to set them up

Another great thing about time stamps is that they count as separate views, thereby increasing your viewer retention rate, e.g. how long people stay on your video.

Viewer retention is one of the most important ranking factors, because it tells Youtube how much viewers liked your video and therefore, how relevant it is to the search phrase (keyword) it ranked for.

Backup

Be sure to keep backups of all your videos. Either on another platform, an external hard drive or services like Dropbox. Channels get deleted every day, so it's best to never just rely on Youtube to save your videos for eternity.

PLANNING

To not get overwhelmed, it is helpful to:

- **Plan your content in advance.** At least the first 10-15 videos. Create thumbnails, research titles and topics.

- **Bulk shoot.** All videos for a week or even an entire month.

Youtube SEO

SEO Basics

If you don't know anything about SEO - the techniques and strategies that help websites and videos rank in Google and Youtube - please read **book 3 of this series**. It will give you a good, solid overview with just an hour's read (a lot less painful than most other Beginner Guides, trust me....;-)

According to most successful Youtubers, THE most effective and fastest strategy to grow your Youtube following is SEO, e.g. people finding you through searches.

They type in a search phrase (= a "keyword" in SEO lingo), see a list of search results on the right and then click on the one that entices them the most. Obviously, the higher up the video, the better the chances of being discovered.

If they like the video, they'll stay for a while and possibly watch more videos of that channel.

If it's not what they're looking for, they will quickly go back to the search results, triggering a negative signal to Youtube that will probably result in that video ranking lower next time.

This is called "bounce rate" and if it happens to the same video a lot, that video will drop lower and lower while other videos move up.

Just like Google, Youtube tries to bring its viewers the most relevant content for each keyword. How long a viewer stays on a video happens to be THE most important factor for Youtube to determine relevance and quality and ranking will happen accordingly.

Occasional bouncing is normal and b

Ranking Factors

- The #1 ranking factor in Youtube is **Watch Time** = how long each viewer stays on your video.

- Connected to Watch Time is **Session Time** = how long a viewer stays on Youtube as a whole - your channel, plus every channel that follows.

Youtube's top priority is to keep viewers on their platform as long as possible, that's why these 2 parameters are the most important for ranking.

How do you ensure long watch time?

Two words:

GREAT CONTENT!

It always comes back to that.

Great content attracts subscribers and views and keeps viewers engaged and watching -> Youtube loves your channel and will promote you more actively, bringing you even more views.

Subscribers add twice as much watch time to your videos on average - not surprisingly, since they already expressed a strong interest.

The next important factors are :

- Exact Keyword in Title

- Tags (= the words and phrases you want to rank for)

- Keyword in the Description

Other factors include:

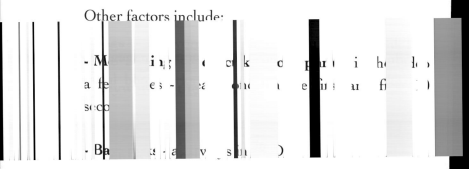

- Engagement - especially comments, shares, embeds, social bookmarks - not so much number of likes or views (you will often see a video with 10K> views rank among videos with 6 figure view counts)

- **Age of the video**. Anything older than 2 years usually doesn't rank as well anymore.

OPTIMIZING YOUR VIDEOs

Aside from watch time and quality content, there are a number of SEO strategies that can greatly help with ranking.

The absolute first and most important is:

Keyword Research

Keywords are the search terms people enter to find a relevant video. For a more in-depth explanation on keyword research, please **check out book 3**, but we'll cover the basics here that you can apply right now:

From the last chapter you already have a basic idea of what you want your keyword/topic to be, and now we will fine tune the exact phrase.

For ranking purposes, we want to use **a phrase of *at least* 3-4 words** - a **"Long Tail" Keyword** as they are called. Those are much easier to rank for.

We are looking for Long Tail keywords with:

- **good search volume** (= how many people per month search for this *exact* term) and

- **low competition** (= not too many other people are trying to rank for the same term)

The fastest, simplest way to do this, is once again, **TubeBuddy** - and

You can see a demo on the Resources page

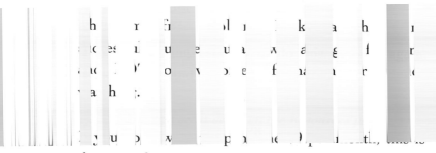

the manual way:

To see search volume in Youtube, simply enter the exact keyword phrase in " ":

Try to stay under 5000 monthly searches in Youtube.

Next, go to the *Google Keyword Planner*, enter your keyword idea and see what other variations come up. Maybe something with better numbers and more suited to your topic? Ideally, try to stay around 500-1000 monthly searches in the beginning.

Once we have narrowed down our exact keyword for this video, we need to optimize the meta data:

Keyword in Title
Use the exact keyword phrase at the beginning of your title and then add something catchy to get users to click. Don't make the title too long. Google cuts titles after 66 characters and adds "Youtube" before the video (taking an extra 10 characters), so try to keep your titles under 50 characters.

No need to use "Video" in the title. It only uses up space and won't help with ranking.

Keyword in Video

Google and Youtube both understand what you say in your videos, so be sure to mention the keyword a few times casually when appropriate. Ideally once in the first 10 seconds and at the end.

You should also double check the auto-generated captions for errors and correct the keyword where needed - or upload your own caption file. Rev.com is a great, inexpensive service at only $1 per minute of footage.

Keyword in the Description

blog post. Obviously, not a transcript, but describe briefly what you will talk about in the video.

Use link shorteners like bit.ly to avoid overly lengthy urls

Do not add tags in the description. It's a violation of Youtube's Terms of Services.

Also add your social media profiles and website links. To make a link clickable in Youtube, always start a url with http://

TAGs

Tags are keywords and keyword variations - other search terms that Youtube will rank you for. You can choose up to 15 (though that number can always change).

Of course, start with your main keyword and also add your name and brand / channel names. For the remaining tags, you can browse some well-converting videos from other channels and see what meta tags they are using to give you some ideas.

Check the Resources for videos on:
- How to Tag
- How to see other user's Tags

Keyword in the Annotations *(not required, but can help Youtube determine what to rank you for)*

Add a keyword annotation in the first 10 seconds of the video and a variation at the end

"How to use Photoshop"

"If you learned something new about how to use Photoshop leave a comment below"

Notice the Call to Action at the end....

Keyword in Caption File
See last chapter

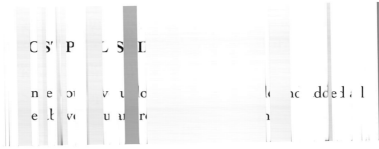

Now it's imperative to get some initial views, shares, comments, etc. to signal Youtube that people are watching and enjoying your video.

Here are a few immediate steps you can take:

- Share on all your other social media platforms and ask others to do the same.

- Build a playlist of related high view count videos (from other channels) and insert your video as the first of the list. Name the playlist after your keyword and add 5-10 other videos. Also fill out the playlist description mentioning the keyword.

- You can even open the video in several different windows and let it play all the way through to get the ball rolling

If you did your keyword research right, you should see your video in the top few pages pretty soon.

Sometimes, right away. Other times it may take a few hours, or even a day, and it will keep climbing in the following weeks.

To give it an extra punch you can buy a few Fiverr or Konker gigs for *(direct links of the Resources Page)*:

- Social Bookmarking

- Embeds

This full service gig can support you with more competitive keywords:

- Complete Video Ranking Gig

And this software boosts up everything else you build and is widely used by SEOs and Youtubers:

- BacklinksIndexer

Strategies to Grow your Following

While quality content and SEO will always be the corner stones of any successful Youtube growth, here are 15 more ways to grow your following.

Lets have a look!

#1 - Publish a *lot* of videos
This one is simple math. The more products you have in your inventory, the more opportunities to be discovered in a Youtube search, especially when you know how to rank for keywords with good search volume.

Having a lot of videos also gives visitors a chance to get to know your channel better. If someone spends time watching several videos or even a whole playlist, they are much more likely to subscribe and be interested in future content.

This also increases your watch and session time, which in turn, will have Youtube promote your channel even more actively.

Of course, quantity has to be met with high quality, otherwise, none of this will work.

#2 - Collaborations

Collaborations with other channels are another great way to introduce new viewers to your work. You'll connect with new audiences, and your viewers will love all the extra value they're getting.

Don't see other channels as competition. You can all help each other and if you remember what I said about session time, then you know that even viewers continuing to another channel after watching your videos, is a good thing, because it all counts towards your channel's total session time.

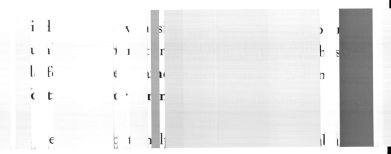

Once you connect your channel, Tubular will analyze your stats and provide you with suggestions for:

- Channels your audience likes
- Subscribers with more than 5K followers
- Influential new subscribers

All great possible collaborator options.

You also want to start building relationships with influencers, but be realistic. That will probably take a little time.

NEVER pitch your channel in comments on other channels. It's considered spam, rude - and will probably get you banned.

Instead, watch their videos and leave valuable comments, ask a question, or answer another viewers' question. Do that consistently and the channel owner will start noticing you and probably take a look at your channel.

If you have really great content, they will eventually be open to collaborate, because your content adds much value to theirs - and sending people to your channel can increase their overall Session time.

#3 - Creator Groups

Build a group of creators and promote each other's content. You can all be each other's street team and everyone benefits. A lot of indie musicians did this with great success.

You can also add each other as "Featured Channels" in your dashboard. That way, everybody gets additional exposure from each of your audiences.

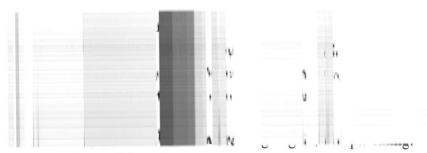

Be useful and fun - and only when appropriate occasionally mention a video.

If you leave interesting comments and help people, they will automatically want to find out more about you and check out your channel.

#5 - Promote across all Social Media
Obviously, use your other social media platforms to strongly promote your videos. Share them and engage by asking questions, feedback to a topic, their opinion.

Ask your friends and followers to share. Especially, when you are brand new, there is no shame in admitting that you need help spreading the word. Youtube is still considered very "cool" and people will be excited for you.

#6 - Playlists
A great way to expand your visibility in search results is to create multiple playlists.

1) For one, it is much easier for new visitors to find what they are looking for when they visit your channel for the first time.

2) Having related videos in a series also encourages extended viewing -> more time spent on your channel.

You can even set up your videos to switch to playlist mode, meaning when someone clicks on your video, the whole playlist will show on the right side.

To set this up, simply link from your End Card or final annotation to the next video in the series.

3) Playlists make it more likely for your videos to show in related searches (on the right). You want video A to lead to Video B and therefore for Video B to show on the right while viewers are still watching video A.

It can help to make the second half of the description

Playlists need to be optimized as well: engaging keyword title, keyword in the playlist description etc. Make it fun and interesting to check out that list.

#7 - Trends & Tags

If a topic is trending and can be related in some way to your channel's overall theme, you could make a video on it.

An example were the mannequin or ice bucket challenges where even brand new channels gained a lot of traction simply by having fun videos that they promoted with trending hashtags and tags.

#8 - Add a hashtag at the end of the Title

The vast majority of Youtubers are tied to their twitter accounts, so when they "like" a video, it also shows in their Twitter feed and will be visible on Twitter for that hashtag.

Example: #Mondaymotivation #thursdaythoughts

#9 - Youtube and Facebook Ads

This one isn't free, but can be very effective.

Check out the article by Neil Patel (link on the Resources Page) to learn how to get the most out of your Youtube Ads

Facebook Ads can also work really well for your Youtube channel, and can be a quick way to get your first viewers and subscribers.

#10 - Interview Influencers

Once you have build a good first following and can boast an inventory of first rate content, an influencer might agree to be interviewed by you - *if* - you have an interesting angle or proposition.

It doesn't take much of their time and they will probably promote that video to their audience, which can be a big boost for you.

#11 - The Nested Strategy

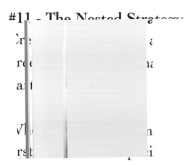

Playlist: Cat Breeds
Video 1: Cat Breeds - Siamese Cats

Video 2: Cat Breeds - Rag Dolls

and so on….

Add "Cat Breeds" to the description, video script, tags and playlist description.

For ranking purposes, this will establish you as a thought leader on the topic of Cat Breeds. Youtube will see you as an authority on the topic and rank you more prominently.

#12 - Use Youtube Analytics

Watch your analytics regularly and see where audiences stay or where they leave.

See a demo video on the Resources Page

Find out why people leave at a particular point. Maybe your energy dropped, or you went on too long on a point? If there are trends, try to analyze them as best you can and then adjust your content accordingly.

Also, remember what we said about the importance of Session Time?

When you notice in your analytics that audiences tend to click away at a certain time stamp, insert a card or annotation right there, inviting them to click away to another video - either one of yours or another channel that you know will probably keep them engaged for a while.

Don's worry about competition, because the time viewers spend on the next channel - possibly binge watching all their videos - gets counted towards YOUR Session Watch Time! - Which is another reason why collaborations are great.

#13 - Your website

Even as a Youtuber you should have a website or blog. For several reasons:

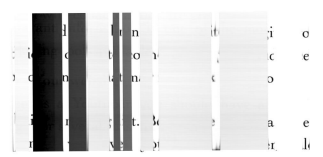

important information is one of the most powerful marketing tools available.

Most of all, you own that list! - No one can take it from you, unlike social media platforms that could always ban you or change their rules.

This way, you have access to your viewers through another independent route, and you don't always have to create a video to contact them.

3) Use your website to promote your Youtube channel. Have a widget in the side bar, embed your videos and include frequent calls-to-action to check out your channel.

If you don't have a website yet - **the first book in this series** will take you through the technical set up - step by step - even if you have no technical knowledge whatsoever. And you don't need to know coding.
It's pretty easy, in fact, more like using Microsoft Word once the basics are set up.

#14 - Channel Trailer
Focus on having a great channel trailer. This is free advertising by Youtube to allow you to introduce your channel in a minute or less. You can also upload it to your Facebook page and - if it's short enough your Twitter and Instagram.

Youtube will use this trailer to promote your channel

#15 - CTAs

We already talked about the importance of frequent calls-to-action throughout your videos, both verbally and through annotations and cards.

This includes asking people to subscribe to your channel at the end of each video, asking for comments, clicking on a link etc.

Find a way to engage them with your content. Let them share their experiences or tips - or questions. *Asking* for a comment will have a much greater result than hoping it will just happen. Engage your viewers whenever you can.

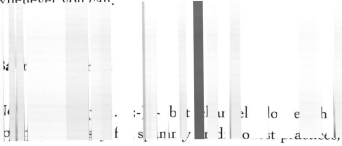

so it's best - and safest - not to engage in:

196

- Overtly driving traffic away from Youtube - for example by mentioning words like "discount" or "Special Offer" in the title with a link to a sale's page. (Those words will get the video deleted and your channel a "Community" strike - the algorithm picks it up instantly)

- Buying likes, views, subscribers (Youtube has become pretty good at detecting those)

- Leaving what is considered spam comments on other channels like asking others to check out your videos, website or affiliate offers. Channel owners will ban you and report you as spam. Your account might get shut down.

If you ever feel stuck…..

If you ever feel stuck and that things are not moving no matter what you try, I recommend watching this video on the Resources page:

29 Ideas for Sparking Growth on your YouTube Channel

How to make Money on Youtube

In this section, we will cover 10 awesome strategies to monetize your Youtube channel and hopefully turn this activity into a full time income eventually.

While Ads and affiliate products may be familiar to most, there are quite a few other options that you may not have thought of:

#1 - Ads on your Videos

Unfortunately, one of the least lucrative ways to monetize your channel. Even with thousands of views

To allow ads to show on your videos you need to first create an Adsense account and then connect that account with your Youtube channel.

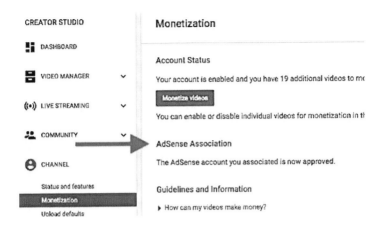

Once completed, you can turn on monetization for each video individually in the video creator tab.

Adsense pay rate is a bit of a mystery and depends on many factors like type of advertiser and product, your genre, and much more.

You can find a great video to shed some light on the Resources page

Since **Youtube Red** allows viewers to enjoy all content ad free, you get paid a percentage based on your view time.

#2 - Affiliate Marketing

Affiliate marketing is a much more lucrative way to monetize your channel.

This is how it works: you recommend a product in your video and then invite viewers to click on the corresponding link in the description to purchase that product. When they do, you get a commission.

The largest store and affiliate place is Amazon and the sign up link can be found in the Resources section.

Once approved you can create special links for each product that you want to promote - with your affiliate ID embedded for tracking.

Be careful though to not create what YouTube
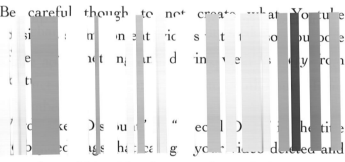

your channel hit with a "community strike".

A strike is a warning and a 1st strike turns off many important features on your channel for 6 months, incl. custom thumbnails, monetization, long videos and others. You definitely want to avoid a strike at all cost!

Instead, you can create a review video that provides valuable information and gives viewers an overview over the product, its features, pros / cons etc. and then mention where people can buy it or try it out.

You can also list the equipment you use (cameras, microphones etc.) in the description of each video, each with their own affiliate link.

Be sure to use a link shortener like **bit.ly** or **Pretty Link** (free Wordpress plugin) to avoid ugly, long urls.

To increase your earnings, apply the same SEO principles as for any other video and pay especially good attention to keyword research as affiliate terms are usually more competitive.

If you find the golden Long Tail "nuggets", you can make a lot of money, pretty much on auto pilot.

Affiliate marketing is a huge topic all on its own and many books have been written about it. It still comes down for the most part to your SEO chops - both in Google and Youtube. Learn SEO well, create great content, headlines and thumbnails - and you can monetize anything!

#3 - Brand Deals & Sponsorships

Produce videos for companies to promote their brand and get paid (sponsored) and/or free products.

Companies will feature you on their social media platforms and drive traffic to your channel, thereby also increasing your viewership and, of course, affiliate commissions.

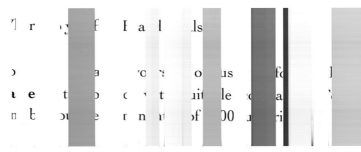

Other companies like **Grapevinelogic** let you start at 1000. Here are a few more options:

Reelio

Izea

ChannelPages

To figure out what you should price your videos, **Social Blue Book** is a great tool, to do the math for you. It is also used by the companies you pitch to, so mentioning that you are using a SocialBlueBook quote will add credibility.

To help you get started, I added a great video series on the Resources page to take you through all the steps of successfully landing brand deals.

#4 Crowdfunding and Donations

Another great way to generate a regular stream of income is Crowdfunding. For Youtube the most widely used platform is **Patreon**.

To entice viewers to become regular monthly donors you can offer a tiered system of perks, bonus material and exclusive content.

Check out the Video Series on Crowdfunding on the Resources page

In January 2017, Youtube introduced its own brand new Crowdfunding feature: **Superchat**, which replaced the former crowdfunding option available through your channel.

With Superchats, viewers can donate to your channel during live streams.

Check out the demo video on the Resources Page

#5 - Sell Products & Merchandise

Youtube offers a very effective way to market your products - both physical and digital (ebooks, virtual courses etc.).

It is much easier and faster to rank in Youtube th

You can wear or place the merchandise in the video somewhere and occasionally pitch it where appropriate.

There is a great video series on the Resources Page to show you how to sell to viewers

#6 - Market your Business

In that same line, Youtube can be a great marketing tool for your business. Most companies these days have a welcome video on their website and it's usually hosted on Youtube.

Same benefits as in #5

#7 - License your Content

If you create visually stunning or cool looking videos, brands may want to use your content in their ads. In this case you would be selling a license to use your content.

#8 - Paid Membership Site

Once you have a loyal following, you can offer more direct access and exclusive content on a paid membership site. A great way to create passive income long term.

Wishlist is a good platform for membership sites.

#10 - Rent & Sell Your Videos

Youtube offers the option to rent out or sell access to some of your videos. You can use this for paid live events (conferences or seminars), previews, exclusive content and much more.

See video on the Resources page for more information

Vlogging

Vlogging is about story telling, more like reality TV vs. "How to" / informational type videos.

Of course, both can overlap, especially in fields like travel blogging, but the story telling aspect, the sharing of someone's life and adventures, is obviously the main reason for people to follow a vlogger.

It would go way beyond the scope of this book to go in-depth on how to start a vlog, but one of the best ways to get started is obviously following a number of successful vloggers and see how they do it.

Watch what their audience responds to. What works and what doesn't and then find your own way.

They also usually have a "How to become a Vlogger" video on their channel and watching a few will give you different perspectives, ideas and strategies.

"**Vlog like a Boss**" is a new bestselling book by vlogger Amy Schmittauer from "Savvy Sexy Social" offering great information and tips.

As for marketing a vlog, it's not much different than any other channel. Most of the principles discussed in this chapter will apply just the same.

Tools & Further Training

(please find direct links on the Resources Page)

- SassyZenGirl.com/Youtube-Resources -

The quickest way to get started is this course:

"TURN YOUTUBE INTO YOUR CAREER"
SassyZenGirl.com/Schmoyer-Course

The Ultimate Youtube Management Tool:

TubeBuddy
The one must have tool for every Youtuber. Starts with a free version.
- Custom Thumbnails and templates
- SEO: Optimize Tags, Description, Titles
- Research topics, titles and keywords
- Bulk Editing for Descriptions, Thumbnails, Annotations etc.
- Direct upload to Facebook
- Best times to upload based on your audience
- Search ranking tool: will tell you how each of your keywords is ranking in real time.

COLLABORATIONS

Tubular - analyzes your channel for networking and collaboration opportunities

OUTROS & INTROS

Outromaker - lets you create intros and outros for your channel.

MUSIC (royalty free)
Paid

Audio Blocks - $99 per year to get unlimited access to a huge selection of tracks and songs. If you produce a lot of videos, this is a great deal

Epidemic Sound - unlimited downloads for $10 per month

InCompetech

CC Mixter - be sure to select "commercial free use"

Josh Woodward - mostly vocal music

COVER & THUMBNAIL DESIGN
TubeBuddy for Thumbnails, see above

Graphical Tube - creates customized cover images for Youtube channels
Canva
PicMonkey
GIMP

Free Photos:
GraphicStock
FreeImages
Creative commons in **Flickr**

SCREEN RECORDING
Screenflow
Camtasia

TRANSCRIPTIONS & CAPTIONS
Rev.com - transcriptions and captions for $1 per minute/translation for 10c per word

SEO Gigs

Social Bookmarking

Embeds

full service gig for more competitive keywords

This software boosts up everything else you build and is widely used by SEOs and Youtubers:

BacklinksIndexer

BRAND DEALS

Famebit

Grapevinelogic

Reelio

Izea

ChannelPages

SocialBlueBook - *to help you price your pitches*

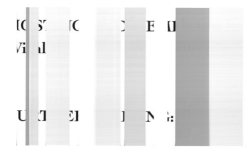

The Top Rated Video Marketing Course....
find the direct link on the Resources page

BOOKS
30 Days to a Better Youtube Channel
Vlog like a Boss

CHANNELS
Derral Eves
Video Creators
Roberto Blake
Video Influencers
Reel SEO
James Wedmore

Daily Routine

NETWORK
Find related channels with similar audiences and start leaving valuable comments on a regular basis. Really watch their videos and have something interesting to say - not just "great content"

Get on their radar without being intrusive. Plus, you can learn a lot about video creation and what content works well....

COLLABORATE

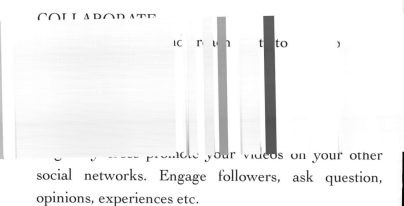

ic r i   t to   )

social networks. Engage followers, ask question, opinions, experiences etc.

PRODUCE

Create a weekly or monthly schedule for your video productions. Many successful Youtubers advise to bulk produce to not get overwhelmed. Try to develop a monthly schedule that includes:

- content research
- Storyboard
- Filming
- Editing
- Thumbnail design
- SEO/Keyword Research
- SEO/Optimizing
- Marketing

Try to add at least 1 new video per week - ideally more.

Final Words

There you have it!

A first overview over the 5 major social media platforms, and the marketing techniques that can help you grow a following quickly.

If all this seems a little overwhelming, just start with one, learn the basics, see what works and how much time you need to invest. And then possibly add a 2nd one.

e : f n
f i e n
v y

ic gave you a better sense of what each platform can achieve, what you need to do to grow, and which might suit you best.

Ideally, the ones you most enjoy using anyway - even in your private life.

Upcoming Trends

Social Media are always changing and evolving and it's important to stay abreast of any trends, new features and updates.

What may have worked 2 years ago, may no longer be valid and unless you know about new, awesome features, you can't really use them....

I highly recommend reading the following 2 articles by two of the top sources on anything related to Social Media marketing, featuring their predictions for 2017:

Social Media Examiner
Buffer

The fastest way to grow an Audience...

To me, the final piece in the puzzle when it comes to online marketing is Kindle Publishing - though it's rarely ever mentioned in that context.

Kindle income is passive income. Once it's set up right and your book is selling, it pretty much pays you every month on auto pilot.

In addition, you are making use of the biggest marketing machine on the planet - Amazon - who will actively promote you and feature your book if it's popular and has a passionate audience.

What's more - it is the easiest and fastest way to build a mailing list - again, on auto pilot!

And....being a published author - possibly even a bestselling author - gives you immediate authority and respect in your field. More than anything else.

So I invite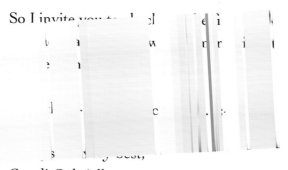

Gundi Gabrielle
SassyZenGirl.com/Freedom

Interested in FREE Books?

Then join the Launch Team and get all my current and future books for free.

As a test reader & reviewer, you will have access to a free review copy of each book you are interested in reading (ebook format). You can choose which books and topics you want to review.

How to apply?

Please send a message with the following information to **contact@SassyZenGirl.com**:

- Link to your Amazon review of this book

- Which of my books have you read so far?

- Can you commit to reading a book within 1 week and give feedback?

- Are you interested in travel or business / internet marketing - or both?

Anything else you'd like to share....

More SassyZenGirl Books:

#1 Bestselling
BEGINNER INTERNET MARKETING
Series

TRAVEL for FREE

a DIGITAL NOMAD BIZ
you can run from anywhere
in the world!

About the Author

Gundi Gabrielle is a 7-time #1 Bestselling Author, Internet Entrepreneur and Digital Nomad.

A former Carnegie Hall conductor and Concert Organist, she decided 3 years ago to make a bold change in her life, packed up a few belongings and drove all the way from Santa Monica, California, to Alaska. She has been traveling ever since and loves exploring this beautiful world without being tied to one place.

She has road tripped through all 50 US States and parts of Canada, lived in several European countries for a number of years and visited most of Europe, as well South America, Southern Africa, Australia, New Zealand and many countries in South East Asia and the Middle East.

She runs the Travel Blog *SassyZenGirl*, writes travel and blogging books and often house or farm sits along her travels, nurturing her love for animals and solitude.

She has no plans of settling down anytime soon…

SassyZenGirl.com

Pinterest.com/SassyZenGirl

GundiGabrielle.com

79404639R00124

Made in the USA
Columbia, SC
23 October 2017